AA/Baedeker
London

D1516361

Baedeker's

AA

London

THE AUTOMOBILE ASSOCIATION

Imprint

Cover picture: Big Ben (Houses of Parliament)

115 colour photographs
9 plans, 1 plan of Underground, 1 large map of central London

Text:
Christa Sturm

Conception and editorial work:
Redaktionsbüro Harenberg, Schwerte
English language:
Alec Court

Cartography:
David L. Fryer & Co., Henley-on-Thames
Ingenieurbüro für Kartographie Huber & Oberländer, Munich
London Transport (plan of Underground)
Hallwag AG, Berne (map of central London)
London Transport Underground Map Registered User Number 83/067

General direction:
Dr Peter Baumgarten, Baedeker Stuttgart

English translation:
James Hogarth

Source of illustrations:
British Tourist Authority (39), dpa (25), Historia-Photo (9), Messerschmidt (1), Retinski (1), Prenzel (1), Sperber (35), ZEFA (1), Museum of London (83), AA Picture Library (95, 151).

Following the tradition established by Karl Baedeker in 1844, sights of particular interest and hotels of outstanding quality are distinguished by either one or two asterisks.

To make it easier to locate the various sights listed in the "A to Z" section of the Guide, their coordinates on the large map of central London are shown in red at the head of each entry.

Only a selection of hotels can be given: no reflection is implied, therefore, on establishments not included.

In a time of rapid change it is difficult to ensure that all the information given is entirely accurate and up to date, and the possibility of error can never be entirely eliminated. Although the publishers can accept no responsibility for inaccuracies and omissions they are always grateful for corrections and suggestions for improvement.

© 1982 Baedeker Stuttgart
Original German edition

© 1982 Jarrold and Sons Ltd
English language edition worldwide

© The Automobile Association, 1982 57150
United Kingdom and Ireland
Revised edition, 1984

Reprinted 1985

Licensed user:
Mairs Geographischer Verlag GmbH & Co., Ostfildern-Kemnat bei Stuttgart

Reproductions:
Gölz Repro-Service GmbH, Ludwigsburg

The name *Baedeker* is a registered trademark

Printed in Great Britain by Jarrold & Sons Ltd Norwich

ISBN 0 86145 120 1

Contents

Preface

This Pocket Guide to London is one of the new generation of Baedeker city guides.

Baedeker pocket guides, illustrated throughout in colour, are designed to meet the needs of the modern traveller. They are quick and easy to consult, with the principal sights described in alphabetical order and practical details about opening times, how to get there, etc., shown in the margin.

Each guide is divided into three parts. The first part gives a general account of the city, its history, population, culture and so on; in the second part the principal sights are described; and the third part contains a variety of practical information designed to help visitors to find their way about and make the most of their stay.

The new guides are abundantly illustrated and contain numbers of newly drawn plans. In a pocket at the back of the book is a large city map, and each entry in the main part of the guide gives the coordinates of the square on the map in which the particular feature can be located. Users of this guide, therefore, will have no difficulty in finding what they want to see.

Facts and Figures

General

London is the capital of the United Kingdom of Great Britain and Northern Ireland, a Parliamentary democracy formed by the union of England and Wales, Scotland and Northern Ireland, with only one land frontier – between Northern Ireland and the Republic of Ireland. As capital of the United Kingdom, London is the residence of the monarch (see Buckingham Palace) and the seat of the government and of Parliament. (The capital of Wales is Cardiff, of Scotland Edinburgh, of Northern Ireland, Belfast. The Channel Islands and the Isle of Man depend directly on the Crown.)

The language of the United Kingdom is English. Since 1967 the Welsh language has enjoyed equal status with English in the administration of justice and the conduct of government business in Wales. French is a second official language in Jersey and Guernsey.

London is situated on the River Thames in SE England, on latitude 50°31′ N. The Greenwich Meridian (0° longitude) runs through the London borough of Greenwich (see entry).

Situation

The original heart of London, the City of London, has an area of only 2·59 sq. km (1 sq. mile) and a resident population of some 5000 (though more than half a million people work there). The County of London, established in 1888, had an area of 303 sq. km (117 sq. miles) and a population of 3·2 million in 1965 when it gave place to an even larger unit formed by the amalgamation of the county of London with the small county of Middlesex and parts of the adjoining counties of Surrey, Essex, Kent and Hertfordshire – Greater London, with an area of 1618 sq. km (625 sq. miles) and a population of more than 6·9 million.

Area and population

In a still wider sense the name of London is applied to the great conurbation, some 201 km (125 miles) across, with a population of over 12 million, which dominates the South-Eastern planning region.

The area of Greater London is divided between the City of London and 32 London boroughs, whose affairs are controlled by largely independent local councils. Twelve of these boroughs, lying closest to the City, are known as the inner London boroughs: Camden, Greenwich, Hackney, Hammersmith, Islington, Kensington and Chelsea, Lambeth, Lewisham, Southwark, Tower Hamlets, Wandsworth, and Westminster. The 20 other boroughs are Barking, Barnet, Bexley, Brent, Bromley, Croydon, Ealing, Enfield, Haringey, Harrow, Havering, Hillingdon, Hounslow, Kingston upon Thames, Merton, Newham, Redbridge, Richmond upon Thames, Sutton and Waltham Forest.

The London boroughs

◀ *One of London's best-known landmarks: Big Ben*

General

The City of London is governed by the Court of Common Council, headed by the Lord Mayor. The Common Council is made up of 159 members elected annually and 26 aldermen (one for each of the 26 wards into which the City is divided), who are elected for life. There are also two sheriffs, elected annually, who have a variety of functions. The Common Council meets in the Guildhall (see entry); the official residence of the Lord Mayor is the Mansion House (see entry). The local government authority for Greater London is the Greater London Council (GLC), which consists of 100 councillors, elected for a four-year term, and 16 aldermen.

The Lord Mayor – the office of which has existed since 1192 – is elected annually by the Companies of the City of London (who also elect the sheriffs, see Guildhall) in accordance with a traditional procedure. He must previously have served as a member of the Common Council, as an alderman and as a sheriff, and must, like the members of the Common Council, have been engaged in business in the City.

The Companies (known as Livery Companies after their traditional liveries or forms of dress) were originally guilds concerned with the various trades – Drapers, Fishmongers, Goldsmiths, Haberdashers, etc. – and they laid down apprenticeship regulations, standards of quality and so on. They are now mainly concerned with various charitable and educational purposes, as well as playing an important part in the government of the City. Only the Goldsmiths, Fishmongers and Vintners still perform some of the original functions of a guild.

The Lord Mayor in ceremonial dress

Transport

London lies on both banks of the Thames some 80 km (50 miles) above its mouth, and has a port, open to seagoing vessels, which ranks among the principal ports of the world, handling a traffic of 45 million tons. In the Middle Ages it was the only port in Britain carrying on trade with every part of the then known world, and this predominance, unchallenged by any other British port, was enhanced by the increasing importance of London as a commercial and industrial centre.

The main development of the Port of London took place in the 19th c. The docks then constructed, like the Royal Victoria and Royal Albert Docks, have now been closed, and in recent years proposals for the redevelopment of much of the area have been under consideration. An example of what can be done to bring fresh life to this run-down part of London is provided by the St Katharine's Dock (see entry).

The docks are administered by the Port of London Authority (established 1908), which is responsible for the whole of the tidal section of the Thames, extending for a distance of 153 km (95 miles) from Teddington Lock to the mouth of the river. The dock installations cover a total area of 16 sq. km (6 sq. miles), with some 58 km (36 miles) of wharves. The stretch known as the Pool of London, between London Bridge and Tower Bridge, can take only the smaller vessels.

The main growth area in the Port of London is the stretch of the river 24–32 km (15–20 miles) downstream from Tower Bridge, with the extensive port installations of Tilbury, a container terminal and London's passenger harbour (lines to South Africa, Australia and the Far East, carrying about 80,000 passengers annually). Still farther downstream are the oil ports of Shellhaven, Thameshaven, Canvey Island and Coryton, which can handle tankers of up to 90,000 tons.

The main export traffic is in motor vehicles, machinery and chemical products. The principal imports are oil, timber and grain.

London has two major airports, Heathrow and Gatwick. Heathrow, 23 km (14 miles) W of the city centre, is the largest international airport, handling over 30 million passengers a year. Gatwick, 48 km (30 miles) S of London, has a large charter traffic; it handles some 9 million passengers a year.

London is also served by two smaller airports at Luton (mainly charter flights) and Stansted. Proposals to develop Stansted into a third major airport have given rise to considerable controversy.

Air freight traffic is increasing steadily. In 1979 Heathrow and Gatwick handled about 500,000 tons of freight.

London has the largest concentration of employed population in Europe (more than 1·5 million workers), and more than a million people travel in from the suburbs every day to work in the city, 843,000 going by rail, 173,000 by car, 143,000 by bus and 9000 by motorbike or bicycle.

Over 7 million passengers a year travel by rail. Most of these commuters have a journey of under 24 km (15 miles), but some 200,000 live farther out. This traffic, concentrated at peak

London buses

hours in the morning and evening, is handled by 15 major stations. Altogether, there are 325 passenger stations in Greater London.

The fastest form of urban transport is the Underground, with its 418 km (260 miles) of track and 279 stations, handling over 2,200,000 passengers every week (Monday–Friday), an annual total of 115 million. The busiest part of the system is a section of the Bakerloo and Northern lines, with 33 trains an hour; the busiest station is Victoria, which is used by 20 million people every year.

The London Underground is the oldest system of its kind in the world. The first trains ran in 1863, using steam traction; the first electric trains were introduced in 1890. A major development of the system began in 1906–7, and it has been still further extended since the last war with the construction of the Victoria and Jubilee lines. During the last war the Underground stations were extensively used as air-raid shelters.

London also has a well-developed network of bus services, with a total length of more than 6436 km (4000 miles). Its 6500 buses (mainly double-deckers) carry more than 4,600,000 passengers a week, an annual total of some 240 million. The route with the most frequent service (36 buses an hour) is No. 109 (Purley–Westminster); the traffic intersection with the highest frequency of buses is Trafalgar Square (516 an hour). In addition to the familiar red double-deckers there are also a smaller number of "Red Arrows" (fast single-decker buses with limited stops) and the Green Line buses which serve the outlying districts and country areas.

The Underground and city bus services are run by a single authority, London Transport. The former tram and trolleybus services have been phased out since the last war.

A series of motorways radiates from London. The M1 runs NW to Leeds, the M2 in the direction of Canterbury, the M3 SW towards Southampton, the M4 W to Bristol and Wales (with a link to Heathrow Airport), the M40 W towards Oxford. Part of the M25 Orbital Motorway is already open.

Motorways and trunk roads

Other important trunk roads are the following:
A1: the old Great North Road to northern England and Scotland
A2: Rochester, Canterbury, Dover
A3: Portsmouth
A4: Windsor, Bristol and Wales
A5: St Albans
A10: Cambridge
A11: Norwich
A12: Southend, Colchester, Harwich and the E coast
A13: Tilbury
A20: Folkestone
A21: Hastings
A22: Eastbourne
A23: Gatwick Airport, Brighton
A24: Horsham
A30: Southampton
A40: Oxford and the West
A41: Birmingham and the North
A127: Southend
A308: Windsor

Population

By the end of the 16th c. London already had a population of over half a million, and was thus by far the largest city in England. Thereafter it continued to increase until it reached the million mark in the early 19th c. From the middle of the century onwards the City of London showed a steady decline in population (130,000 in 1851, 50,600 in 1881, 13,700 in 1921, 11,000 in 1931 and now only about 5000), while the population of Greater London grew from 2·2 million in 1841 to its present figure of over 8·3 million. This great increase in population not only involved a steady outward extension of the built-up area but led to the creation of satellite towns – Welwyn Garden City (1920) and a series of "new towns" formally established since the last war (Basildon, Bracknell, Crawley, Harlow, Hatfield, Hemel Hempstead and Stevenage).

London's increasing importance as an industrial and commercial centre attracted numerous immigrants and other incomers. In the 17th c. many Huguenots came from France; in the 18th c. there were numerous Irish immigrants; in the early 19th c. many Africans and Chinese settled in London's dockland; after 1880 there was an influx of Jewish families to the East End; after the last war there was a flood of immigrants from the West Indies, Africa, Cyprus, India and Pakistan; and in more recent years numbers of Arabs have established themselves in London, buying hotels and office blocks and

13

making their influence felt in the business world. London and the surrounding area now have the largest concentration of coloured people in the United Kingdom.

Many of these population groups tend to be concentrated in particular parts of London – Jamaicans in Brixton, Trinidadians in Notting Hill, Indians in the East End and in Southall, Chinese in Soho (restaurants and foodshops being a major source of income). Wealthy Arabs show a preference for Kensington.

This influx of immigrants has given rise to social tensions and to a variety of problems (educational and cultural provision for immigrant groups, difficulties over certain religious observances, etc.) which are causing concern to central and local government authorities.

Religion

The religions practised in London are as varied as the ethnic composition of its population. The established Church is the Church of England, of which the Queen is the temporal "head" and to which 66% of the population nominally belong. (In Scotland the established Church is the Church of Scotland, a Presbyterian Church which is also represented in London.)

London is the seat of an Anglican bishop and a Roman Catholic archbishop (there are about 5 million Roman Catholics in Britain). In addition there are churches for Methodists, Baptists, Congregationalists and Presbyterians (with a total of some 1·7 million adherents in Britain, in addition to 1 million members of the Church of Scotland), synagogues for Jews (of whom there are 400,000 in Britain), mosques for Arabs (of whom there are 30,000 in Britain, mostly in London) and other Mohammedans, and a variety of churches, temples and meeting-places for other religions and denominations.

Culture

London is Britain's principal cultural centre and its largest centre of scholarship and learning. The headquarters of the national broadcasting corporation, the BBC, are in London, and almost all the national daily and Sunday newspapers are published in London, with the English provincial press playing a subordinate role. The city has five major orchestras (Royal Philharmonic, London Philharmonic, BBC Symphony Orchestra, the Philharmonia and London Symphony Orchestra), more than 50 theatres (including the famous companies of the National Theatre and the Royal Shakespeare Company, housed in the new Barbican Arts Centre), the largest opera-house in Britain (the Royal Opera House, Covent Garden) and two well-known ballet companies, the Royal Ballet and the London Festival Ballet. (See Practical Information, Music.)

London also has the country's leading museums, including the British Museum, the Victoria and Albert and the Natural History Museum (see entries), art galleries of international reputation, among them the National Gallery and Tate Gallery (see entries), together with other important galleries such as the Hayward Gallery (see entry) and the Institute of Contemporary Arts, and one of the great libraries of the world, the British Library (see British Museum).

London: a melting-pot of nations and races

The University of London, which was originally founded in 1836 as an examining body and which became a teaching university in 1900, now has over 42,000 students. The University, with nine faculties, consists of a number of largely autonomous colleges and schools (some of them with several faculties) in various parts of London and the surrounding counties. London University was the first university to grant degrees to women (in 1878).

The main buildings of the University lie just W of Russell Square, dominated by the massive tower which contains the Senate House and University Library. N of this, in Gower

University of London

Street, is the largest college, University College (founded 1826). King's College occupies one wing of Somerset House (see entry). Other colleges belonging to the University or associated with it are Bedford College (see Regent's Park), the Imperial College of Science and Technology (South Kensington), the London School of Economics (LSE, near Kingsway), Birkbeck College and Goldsmith's College.

Two other universities were established in London in the 1960s, the City University with over 2400 students, and Brunel, with over 1700. In addition there are various colleges of technology, the London Business School (which has university status), art colleges (Chelsea School of Arts, Royal College of Art), the Royal Naval College (see Greenwich) and numerous research institutes.

Commerce and Industry

London's position as the capital of a world empire gave it international importance as a centre of diplomatic and economic activity, and at least until the First World War it was the world's leading financial centre. In the field of marine and air insurance (Lloyd's) it still retains its dominant position.

The London Stock Exchange is one of the world's leading exchanges. Since the last war two great auction houses, Sotheby's and Christie's (see Practical Information, Auction rooms) have made London a major international centre of the art trade.

As capital of the United Kingdom, London is the administrative, commercial and industrial centre of the country. More than 27% of all employed persons engaged in administration, and more than 20% of those employed in industry, work within the area of Greater London. Here, too, are the headquarters of all the leading industrial firms, and major industrial and commercial organisations; London's various exhibition halls house numerous trade fairs and exhibitions of national and international importance.

While the development of industry in and around London is now tending to stagnate, its importance as a centre of administration, commerce and the service industries continues to increase. The main concentration of business firms is still in the City of London, now a district of towering office blocks. One of the largest of its new buildings is the Stock Exchange.

Traditional industries

The development of London's industry has been influenced by four main factors – its position as the national capital, the availability of a large labour force, the large market offered by this concentration of population and the proximity of a major port.

The city's traditional industries are the manufacture of clothing and furniture, and the printing trade (with a virtual monopoly of the British press). Another old-established trade is diamond-cutting, concentrated in Hatton Garden. Precision engineering (developed out of the older trade of clockmaking) and the electrical industries have largely migrated to new industrial areas.

The new Stock Exchange, flanked by the Bank of England and the Royal Exchange ▶

The existence of the Port of London led to the development of an industrial zone in the 19th c., with woodworking and furniture manufacture, sugar refineries and other foodstuffs industries (e.g. brewing) and the chemical industries.

New industries

Between the two world wars cement-making, papermaking and car manufacture (Ford's, Dagenham) were established on the lower reaches of the Thames. Since the end of the last war a major development has been the establishment of a large refinery and industrial complex (petrochemicals) at Tilbury (see Port of London).

Parliament

Government authority in the United Kingdom is vested in Parliament (the House of Lords and the House of Commons acting together), with the assent of the monarch, and the country's government is carried on in the name of the Queen. This constitutional position is expressed in two traditional formulas – "The Queen in Parliament", as the seat of sovereignty, and "Her Majesty's Government" as the designation of the executive.

Historical development

This concept of cooperation between the monarch and a free assembly, representing every part of the country, was already in operation in Anglo-Saxon times, in the form of the Witenagemot (a free, though not an elected, assembly). The Witenagemot could choose the king and could depose him; and only with its agreement was the king able to make and promulgate laws, appoint bishops and high dignitaries, make grants of land, levy taxes, make war or conclude peace and establish a supreme criminal and civil court. It was thus an assembly in which supreme legislative and judicial authority were combined.

The Norman kings introduced the Great Council, made up of the king's immediate feudal vassals, which advised him in the performance of his legislative function; in the course of time this developed into the bodies representing the whole nation which we know as Parliament. Thus in 1215 King John was compelled by a group of 25 barons to sign Magna Carta, which required him to secure the assent of the "Common Council" before levying taxes. This Council consisted of prelates, members of great noble families, who were summoned by name, and feudal landholders appointed by the sheriffs.

In 1254 the sheriff of each shire (county) was invited to send to the Council four knights elected by the shire. This marked the introduction of the representative system.

In 1265 the cities and boroughs also sent representatives (the "commons") to the Great Council.

Parliament

A further important stage was marked by Edward I's "Model Parliament" in 1295. This consisted of archbishops, bishops and abbots together with a number of lay nobles (7 earls and 41 barons, all listed by name). The prelates were invited to

State Opening of Parliament ▶

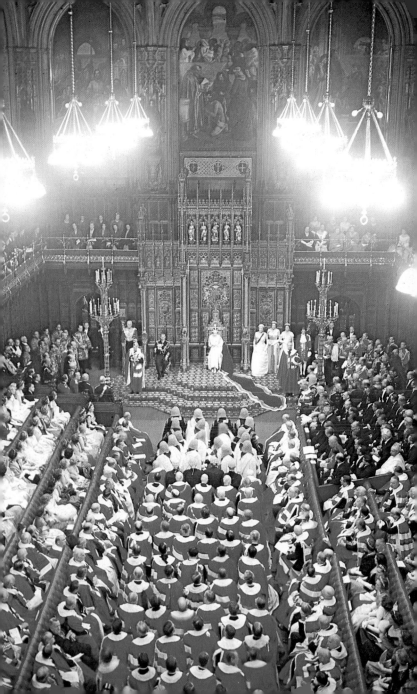

bring representatives of the lower clergy with them, and the sheriffs were required to arrange for the election of two knights from each shire, two citizens from each city and two burgesses from each borough. Parliament was thus no longer a purely feudal body, but one representing the main groups in the country. Its two main functions were to act as a supreme court of justice (the "High Court of Parliament") and to give assent to taxes – a power which developed into its right to agree to laws proposed by the king.

The separation into two houses took place in the middle of the 14th c., when the knights of the shires met together with the representatives of the cities and boroughs as the "Commons of England", while the ecclesiastical and temporal lords met separately.

From the time of Henry VIII it became the accepted rule that Parliament could address petitions to the king, which he could either agree to or reject. Thereafter the conflicts between king and Parliament, which ended in the execution of Charles I, were concerned solely with the question of whether sovereignty resided in the king alone or in the "King in Parliament"; and eventually the view prevailed that the king and Parliament must be associated in the government of the country.

After the Commonwealth, which followed the execution of Charles I, his successor, Charles II, was summoned to the throne by Parliament; so, too, was William III, who agreed to the Bill of Rights declaring once again that the monarch was subject to the law. The king was not, except with the assent of Parliament, entitled to suspend laws or grant exemption from their provisions, to raise money or to maintain a standing army in peacetime (for which purpose a specified sum of money was to be granted annually by Parliament). Both houses of Parliament were to be free to express their views without fear of reprisals, and the people of the country were to have the right to decide who should succeed to the throne. Thus all theories that the sovereign occupied the throne by divine right were rejected; and all subsequent monarchs have reigned on the basis of an Act of Parliament, following the promulgation of the Bill of Rights in 1689 and the Act of Settlement in 1701, which regulated the succession to the throne. Britain had thus become a constitutional monarchy, and the previous rivalry between Crown and Parliament gave place to a cooperation in which Parliament had the major role.

The monarchy

The United Kingdom is a hereditary monarchy. On the death of the monarch the crown passes to his or her son, or, failing a son, to a daughter. The monarch must be a member of the Church of England (when in Scotland a member of the Church of Scotland), and his or her spouse must not be a Roman Catholic. The monarch can abdicate under the authority of an Act of Parliament.

Since the middle of the 19th c. the monarch's role has been almost entirely confined to representative and ceremonial functions. Political acts – such as the Speech from the Throne at the opening of Parliament – must express the policy of the government, and participation in legislation is of a purely formal nature. The right to be consulted about all government decisions, which still existed at the beginning of the 19th c., has been reduced to a right to be informed (by seeing Cabinet minutes and other documents, etc.). The monarch is required to be neutral in the party-political sense.

The House of Lords – a designation first introduced in the 16th c. – is the upper house of Parliament. It is the oldest and numerically the largest legislative chamber in the world, successor to the Great Council and the representative Parliaments of 1265 and 1295 (which also included the Commons). In the 14th c. the Lords (the higher clergy and nobility) were separated from the Commons; and after the dissolution of the monasteries by Henry VIII the temporal peers became dominant over the ecclesiastical members of the House of Lords.

House of Lords

The Reform Act of 1832, by extending the franchise, deprived the great landowners in the House of Lords of their patronage over seats in the Commons. The Parliament Act of 1911 substantially reduced the role of the Lords in the legislative process: their veto on financial legislation ("money Bills") was now to be effective only for one month, and on all other Bills for two years (a period further reduced to one year in 1949).

The Cabinet system of government has also tended to weaken the position of the House of Lords. It is usual for some Cabinet ministers to be members of the Lords in order to represent the government in that House, but the Prime Minister and the principal members of the Cabinet always sit in the Commons.

The House of Lords contains no elected representatives. Its membership consists of hereditary peers who have acquired their title either by inheritance or by ennoblement; 26 bishops of the Church of England (including the two archbishops); the Lords of Appeal in Ordinary appointed under the Appellate Jurisdiction Act of 1876 to carry out the judicial functions of the House; and peers appointed for life, with no hereditary rights, under the Life Peerage Act of 1958 (which also allowed peeresses to sit in the House). Under the Peerage Act of 1963 it became possible for hereditary peers to disclaim their titles and become eligible for membership of the House of Commons: among peers who have taken this course have been the Earl of Home (Sir Alec Douglas-Home) and Lord Stansgate (Mr Tony Benn).

The present membership of the House of Lords is about 1080 (about a hundred of whom have not applied for a writ of summons), including some 200 life peers, the 16 Lords of Appeal and the 26 bishops. The House is presided over by the Lord Chancellor, who is a member of the government.

Although the House of Lords has long since lost its importance as a source of supply of ministers, it still plays an important part in the critical examination of legislation passed by the House of Commons and the initiation of amendments, as well as in the initial consideration of non-controversial Bills. It also serves as a useful forum for the ventilation of a variety of matters of domestic or international concern.

The House of Lords is the supreme court of appeal for England and Wales and (in civil cases only) Scotland. In this capacity its membership consists of the Lord Chancellor, the Lords of Appeal in Ordinary (the "law lords") and peers who hold or have held high judicial office.

The House of Commons is the second chamber of Parliament. First represented in Parliament in 1265 and 1295, the members

House of Commons

21

of the Commons secured in 1377 the right to elect from among their number a Speaker to present their views to the monarch. The Speaker's role as chairman of the House of Commons is first recorded in 1547, when records of the deliberations began to be kept (see Houses of Parliament).

In the 15th c. the House of Commons gained control of financial legislation, and in the 17th c. it acquired the right to initiate fiscal measures. During the 18th c. Cabinet government came into being, and after an election in 1784 the Parliamentary system of government was established, although until 1832 the monarch's assent to the appointment of the Cabinet was still required.

Until the 19th c. the House of Commons was by no means representative of the population as a whole, given the restricted franchise and the outdated pattern of constituencies. There were steady extensions of the franchise under a series of reforming Acts of Parliament (1832, 1867, 1884, 1885), culminating in the introduction of universal suffrage (including women for the first time) in 1918.

The House of Commons has a membership of 650, made up of 524 for England, 38 for Wales, 71 for Scotland and 17 for Northern Ireland. The distribution of seats at the last election (1983) was Conservatives 396, Labour 209, Liberal 17, Social Democratic Party 6, Scottish National Party 2, Welsh National Party 2, Official Unionist (Northern Ireland) 11, Democratic Unionist (Northern Ireland) 3, Ulster Popular Unionist 1, Social Democratic and Labour (Northern Ireland) 1, Provisional Sinn Fein 1, Speaker 1. The Social Democratic Party was formed in 1981 as a result of internal divisions in the Labour Party.

The government

The government consists of over 100 ministers, mostly members of the House of Commons but including some peers. About 20 of the leading members of the government form the Cabinet, under the leadership of the Prime Minister. Some key ministers (the Chancellor of the Exchequer, the Foreign, Home and Defence Secretaries, and the Lord Chancellor) are always in the Cabinet, but otherwise the Prime Minister is free to decide which ministers should be members of the Cabinet.

The leader of the majority party in the House of Commons is invited by the monarch to form a government and to submit the names of ministers for formal royal appointment. It is the Prime Minister, however, who selects the members of the government and determines the broad lines of policy; and it is the Prime Minister who has the right to dissolve the House of Commons and call a general election.

Following the victory of the Conservative party in the general election of May 1979 Mrs Margaret Thatcher became Britain's first woman Prime Minister.

The leader of the principal opposition party in the House of Commons is known as the Leader of His or Her Majesty's Opposition and receives a salary in recognition of the constitutional importance of his post.

State Opening of Parliament

The opening of each annual session of Parliament is a great ceremonial occasion. The monarch drives to Parliament in the Irish State Coach, attended by Yeomen of the Guard and with an escort of the Household Cavalry; then, wearing robes of

House of Commons

state and crown, walks in procession to the House of Lords, preceded by heralds, officers of the court, the great officers of state and two peers, one bearing on a cushion the red velvet Cap of Maintenance (the significance of which has been forgotten), the other bearing aloft the Sword of State.

In the House of Lords the peers wear their scarlet robes trimmed with ermine. The monarch is seated on the throne, flanked by members of the royal family, and then the Gentleman Usher of the Black Rod, an officer of the House of Lords, is sent to summon the Commons. When he reaches the House of Commons the door is slammed in his face, in order to demonstrate that the Crown has no right of access to the House, and he must knock three times on the door with his staff before being admitted. He then delivers his message commanding the attendance of the Commons in the House of Lords.

Finally, when both houses of Parliament are assembled, the monarch reads the Speech from the Throne, announcing government policies and proposals for the coming session.

Kings and Queens

(Only those Anglo-Saxon kings who ruled the whole of England are listed.)

England
Anglo-Saxon kings

Edwy (Edwin)	955–959
	(from 957 confined to Wessex
Edgar	959–975

Kings and Queens

	Edward the Martyr	975–978
		(Wessex only)
	Ethelred II	978/79–1013
	Swein Forkbeard of Denmark	1013–14
	Cnut (Canute) I, the Great	1016–35
	Edmund Ironside	1016
	Harold I, Harefoot	1035/6–40
	Harthacnut	1040–2
	Edward the Confessor	1042–66
	Harold II Godwinson	Jan.–Oct. 1066
	(Edgar II, the Atheling)	(1066)
Norman kings	William I, the Conqueror	1066–87
	William II (Rufus)	1087–1100
	Henry I (Beauclerc)	1100–35
	Stephen	1135–54
House of Plantagenet	Henry II (Curtmantle)	1154–89
	Richard I (Lionheart)	1189–99
	John (Lackland)	1199–1216
	Henry III	1216–72
	Edward I	1272–1307
	Edward II	1307–27
	Edward III	1327–77
	Richard II	1377–99
House of Lancaster	Henry IV	1399–1413
	Henry V	1413–22
	Henry VI	1422–61
House of York	Edward IV	1461–83
		(in prison and exile 1469–71
	Edward V	1483
	Richard III	1483–5
House of Tudor	Henry VII	1485–1509
	Henry VIII	1509–47
	Edward VI	1547–53
	Mary I	1553–8
	Elizabeth I	1558–1603
United Kingdom House of Stuart	James I	1603–25
	Charles I	1625–49
Commonwealth and Protectorate	Oliver Cromwell (Protector)	1653–8
	Richard Cromwell (Protector)	1658–9
House of Stuart	Charles II	1660–85
	James II	1685–8
	Mary II and William III (of Orange)	1689–1702
	Anne	1702–14
House of Hanover	George I	1714–27
	George II	1727–60
	George III	1760–1820
	George IV	1820–30
	William IV	1830–7
	Victoria	1837–1901

Edward VII	1901–10	House of Saxe-Coburg
George V	1910–36	House of Windsor
Edward VIII	1936	
George VI	1936–52	
Elizabeth II	from 1952	

History of London

Chronology

During the reign of the Emperor Claudius the Roman army conquers Britain, establishes it as a new province, garrisoned by four legions, and founds the trading station of Londinium on the N bank of the Thames.	A.D. 43
Londinium becomes capital of one of the four provinces now formed in Britain.	from 240
Carausius, admiral of the fleet defending Britain against the Saxons, rises against Diocletian, gains control of Britain and has himself proclaimed Emperor, with Londinium as his capital.	286–287
Britain, abandoned by Rome, is overrun by Jutes, Angles and Saxons.	449
Under Anglo-Saxon rule London becomes a royal residence.	796
Union of the Anglo-Saxon kingdoms under Egbert, king of Wessex.	827
London assumes the role of capital. The Anglo-Saxon kings Cnut (Canute, 1016–35) and Edward the Confessor (1042–66) reside at Westminster.	1016–66
After his victory at Hastings, William the Conqueror is crowned in Westminster Abbey.	1066
During the reign of Henry I, London is finally established as the capital and asserts its independence and right of self-government as a kind of city republic subject only to the king.	1100–35
The Norman kings are succeeded by the House of Plantagenet.	1154
Establishment of a Hanseatic trading station on the banks of the Thames.	1157
Richard I grants the citizens of London a charter establishing their rights over traffic on the Thames, and receives in return a payment of £1500.	1189–99

History of London

1192	The office of Lord Mayor, elected by the city companies (see General, Election of Lord Mayor), is instituted.
13th c.	Large religious houses established by Dominicans, Carmelites and Carthusians on the outskirts of the town.
1245–69	Rebuilding of Westminster Abbey in Gothic style.
1272–1307	Inns of Court established during the reign of Edward I. Ecclesiastics are excluded from practice in the lawcourts.
1312	Dissolution of the order of Templars. Their London establishment, the Temple, becomes a law school.
1332	Parliament is divided into two chambers (see General, Parliament).
1483	Richard III secures the throne and, it is said, has his nephews, Edward V and Richard, murdered in the Tower.
1485	The first of the Tudor kings, Henry VII, accedes to the throne.
16th c.	The economic growth of London is accelerated by the establishment of the first trading companies.
1509–47	Establishment of the Church of England during the reign of Henry VIII. Dissolution of the monasteries.
1603	Accession of James I, first of the Stuart kings.
1605	Guy Fawkes and other Roman Catholic conspirators try to blow up Parliament (the Gunpowder Plot).
1649	Charles I is beheaded in Whitehall. Establishment of the Commonwealth; Oliver Cromwell becomes Lord Protector.
1660	Restoration of the Stuarts (Charles II). The population of London reaches the half-million mark.
1665	The Great Plague claims 68,500 victims in London.
1666	The Great Fire devastates four-fifths of the city, destroying 13,200 houses and 89 churches.
1675–1711	Sir Christopher Wren rebuilds St Paul's Cathedral and 50 other churches.
1694	Foundation of the Bank of England (see entry).
1714	The Stuarts are succeeded on the throne by the House of Hanover (George I).
1760	The City's walls and gates are pulled down, and it expands in the direction of Westminster.
1801	The first national census shows London's population to be 860,035.
1808–28	Development of the Port of London makes it Britain's largest port.

Establishment of the Metropolitan Police.	1830
London's first train service, from London Bridge to Greenwich.	1836
During the reign of Queen Victoria London expands faster than ever before, largely as a result of the development of railways. Even the lower-income groups can now live farther from their place of work: London is surrounded by a wide ring of Victorian suburbs.	1837–1901
Queen Victoria makes Buckingham Palace the principal royal residence.	1837
Building of the new Houses of Parliament.	1840–52
The Great Exhibition, housed in Sir Joseph Paxton's Crystal Palace.	1851
The Covent Garden Opera House is built.	1858
Second Great Exhibition.	1862
First Underground line opened between Bishop's Road and Farringdon.	1863
Queen Victoria's Diamond Jubilee.	1897
Accession of George V, first sovereign of the House of Windsor.	1910
First World War. German air raids kill 670 people in London and injure more than 2000.	1914–18
First Zeppelin raid on London.	1915
Second World War. More than 30,000 people are killed in German bombing raids, and the City of London is almost completely destroyed.	1939–45
The "blitz": Londoners are exposed to 57 successive nights of bombing.	1940
Celebrations all over London on VE Day when Germany is finally defeated.	1945
Queen Elizabeth II is crowned in Westminster Abbey.	1953
Reorganisation of local government in London.	1965
Celebrations in London for Queen Elizabeth II's Jubilee (25 years on the throne).	1977
Celebrations in London for the marriage of the Prince of Wales and Lady Diana Spencer.	1981

Quotations

Edmund Burke
(1729–97)

"The buildings are very fine; it may be called the sink of vice, but for her hospitals and charitable institutions, whose turrets pierce the skies, like so many electrical conductors averting the very wrath of heaven . . . An Englishman is cold and distant at first; he is very cautious even in forming an acquaintance . . . The women are not quite so reserved; they consult their glasses to the greatest advantage . . ."

François-René de Chateaubriand
(1768–1848)

"Kensington particularly appealed to me. While the part bordering on Hyde Park was filled with fashionable strollers, I wandered in the solitary park. The contrast between my poverty and this wealth, between my loneliness and this crowd, struck me agreeably. I watched from afar the young English girls walking by. Did anyone pay any attention to the foreigner sitting under a pine-tree?" ("Mémoires d'Outre-Tombe")

Thomas Carlyle
(1795–1881)

"Chelsea is a singular heterogeneous kind of spot, very dirty and confused in some places, quite beautiful in others, abounding with antiquities and the traces of great men."

Giacomo Girolamo Casanova
(1725–98)

(First impressions of England)
"I was struck immediately by the extreme cleanliness, the high quality of the food, the beauty of the landscape and the excellent roads. I admired the fine coaches supplied at the post-houses to those travelling without their own carriage, the reasonableness of the fares, the easy method of payment, the rapid trot, never rising to a gallop, at which the horses travel, and the layout of the towns through which we passed on the way from Dover to London."

Conan Doyle
(1859–1930)

(Sherlock Holmes and Watson in Baker Street)
"We met next day as he had arranged, and inspected the rooms at No. 221B Baker Street of which he had spoken at our meeting. They consisted of a couple of comfortable bedrooms and a single large airy sitting-room, cheerfully furnished and

Chateaubriand

Edmund Burke

Friedrich Engels

Theodor Fontane

John Galsworthy

Heinrich Heine

illuminated by two broad windows. So desirable in every way were the apartments, and so moderate did the terms seem when divided between us, that the bargain was concluded upon the spot, and we at once entered into possession." ("A Study in Scarlet")

"Empress of towns, exalt in honour;
In beauty bearing the crown imperial;
Sweet paradise precelling in pleasure:
London, thou art the flower of cities all."

William Dunbar
(1465?–1530?)

"I know nothing more imposing than the view which the Thames affords when you sail up the river from the sea towards London Bridge. The masses of houses, the wharves on both sides, the countless ships: it is all so magnificent, on such a massive scale, that you are quite lost in astonishment at the greatness of England even before treading English soil."

Friedrich Engels
(1820–95)

"London made an indelible impression on me: I was astonished both by its beauty and its magnificence. It is the model or quintessence of a whole world."

Theodor Fontane
(German novelist, 1819–98)

"Of all quarters in the queer adventurous amalgam called London, Soho is perhaps least suited to the Forsyte spirit . . . Untidy, full of Greeks, Ishmaelites, cats, Italians, tomatoes, restaurants, organs, coloured stuffs, queer names, people looking out of upper windows, it dwells remote from the British Body Politic." ("Forsyte Saga")

John Galsworthy
(1867–1933)

"Send a philosopher to London, but whatever you do, don't send a poet! Send a philosopher there and set him at a street corner in Cheapside: he will learn more than he would from all the books at the last Leipzig Fair, and as the waves of humanity swirl round him a whole ocean of new ideas will surge up in front of him. The eternal spirit which hovers above the city will breathe over him, and the most hidden secrets of the social order will suddenly be revealed to him; he will feel the very pulse-beat of the world.
But do not send a poet to London! This utter seriousness, this colossal sameness, this machine-like movement, this morose-

Heinrich Heine
(1797–1856)

Quotations

ness even in pleasure, this whole overwrought city oppresses the fancy and rends the heart."

Henry James
(1843–1916)

"Nowhere is there such a play of light and shade, such struggle of sun and smoke, such aerial gradations and confusions. To eyes addicted to such contemplations this is a constant diversion, and yet this is only a part of it. What completes the effect of the place is its appeal to the feelings, made in so many ways, but made, above all, by agglomerated immensity. At any given point London looks huge; even in narrow corners you have a sense of its hugeness, and petty places acquire a certain interest from their being parts of so mighty a whole."

Dr Samuel Johnson
(1709–84)

"If you wish to have a just notion of the magnitude of this city, you must not be satisfied with seeing its great streets and squares, but must survey the innumerable little lanes and courts. It is not in the showy evolutions of buildings, but in the multiplicity of human habitations which are crowded together, that the wonderful immensity of London consists."
(5 July 1763)
"When a man is tired of London, he is tired of life; for there is in London all that life can afford."
(20 September 1777)

Charles Lamb
(1775–1834)

"I have passed all my days in London, until I have formed as many and as intense local attachments as any of you mountaineers can have done with dead nature. The lighted shops of the Strand and Fleet Street; the innumerable trades, tradesmen and customers, coaches, waggons, playhouses; all the bustle and wickedness round about Covent Garden; the watchmen, drunken scenes, rattles; – life awake, if you awake, at all hours of the night; the impossibility of being dull in Fleet Street; the crowds, the very dirt and mud, the sun shining upon houses and pavements, the print-shops, the old book-stalls, parsons cheapening books, coffee-houses, steams of soups from kitchens, the pantomimes – London itself a pantomime and a masquerade – all these things work themselves into my mind, and feed me without a power of satiating me."
(Letter to Wordsworth, 30 January 1801)

George Bernard Shaw   *Percy Bysshe Shelley*   *William Wordsworth*

(In a letter written from his flat in Whitehall Court to the actress Molly Tompkins)
"This place is rather wonderful at night with its post in the skies and its panorama of the river from St Paul's to Westminster. When the roads are black wet and the embankment lights and car headlights are pouring floods of gold down them there is really nothing like it in the world."

George Bernard Shaw
(1856–1950)

"Hell is a city much like London – A populous and smoky city."
("Peter Bell the Third")

Percy Bysshe Shelley
(1792–1882)

"Earth has not anything to show more fair:
Dull would he be of soul who could pass by
A sight so touching in its majesty:
This City now doth, like a garment, wear
The beauty of the morning; silent, bare,
Ships, towers, domes, theatres and temples lie
Open unto the fields, and to the sky;
All bright and glittering in the smokeless air."
(Sonnet composed upon Westminster Bridge)

William Wordsworth
(1770–1850)

London from A to Z

Albert Hall C4

Address
Kensington Gore, SW7

Underground station
South Kensington

This large concert hall, also used for public meetings, balls and other events, was built in 1867–71. Its full name is the Royal Albert Hall of Arts and Sciences, and it is a memorial to Queen Victoria's Prince Consort, who had originally proposed its construction.

The hall, designed by Captain Francis Fowke and General Scott, is oval in plan, with a circumference of 198 m (650 ft). It was hailed by contemporaries as a noble building, worthy of Rome in its golden age – a judgment not wholly confirmed by later generations. Although originally noted for its poor acoustics – a defect which was later put right – this huge amphitheatre with its great glass dome has developed over the years into one of London's most popular concert halls. The famous "Proms" (promenade concerts: see Practical Information, Music) take place here every year.

Albert Memorial C4

Situation
Kensington Gore, SW7

Underground station
South Kensington

This memorial to Prince Albert of Saxe-Coburg-Gotha (1819–61), Queen Victoria's consort, in Kensington Gardens (see Kensington Palace), was designed by Sir George Gilbert Scott and unveiled by the Queen in 1876.

The Queen had originally thought of a huge monolithic granite obelisk, to be financed by public subscription, but the amount collected was insufficient and the present more modest monument, in the neo-Gothic style of the period, was built instead.

Albert is seated under a richly decorated canopy 53 m (175 ft) high, holding in his hand the catalogue of the Great Exhibition of 1851. Around the pedestal are 178 marble neo-classical reliefs of artists and men of letters of every period. At the corners of the pedestal are sculptured groups symbolising Manufactures, Engineering, Commerce and Agriculture, and at the outer corners of the steps are other groups symbolising the continents of Europe, Asia, Africa and America.

*All Hallows by the Tower Church K3

Address
Byward Street, EC3

Underground station
Tower Hill

Originally founded in 675, it was rebuilt in the 13th–15th c., badly damaged by bombing in the Second World War and restored in 1957.

The Saxon period is represented by the remains of a 7th c. arch and a cross. The crypt (undercroft) dates from the 14th c. The brick tower (1658) is an example of Cromwellian ecclesiastical architecture; the spire was added in 1959.

Royal Albert Hall

Albert Memorial

All Hallows by the Tower

All Souls' Church

Opening times
Mon.–Fri. 9 a.m.–5.30 p.m.
Sat. and Sun. 10.30 a.m.–
5.30 p.m.

Conducted tours
(seen only with guides)

Admission charge

Notable features are the statues of St Ethelburga and Bishop Lancelot Andrewes (who was baptised in the church) above the N porch (1884), a 16th c. Spanish crucifix in the S aisle and a number of 15th–17th c. tombs. The new font (1944) is carved from stone from Gibraltar.

The Undercroft Museum contains a model of Roman London and various Roman and Saxon remains. The parish registers record the baptism (1644) of William Penn, founder of the state of Pennsylvania, and the marriage of John Quincy Adams, sixth President of the United States. The church had the finest collection of memorial brasses (14th–17th c.) in London. In a memorial chapel is a crusading altar which originally stood in Richard I's castle at Athlit in northern Palestine.

There is a service in the church every Sunday at 11 a.m.

All Souls' Church   F3

Address
Langham Place, Regent
Street, W1

Underground station
Oxford Circus

The church, built by John Nash in 1822–4, has a circular portico and a tower surrounded by a ring of freestanding columns, with a slender spire which was designed to form a vertical feature closing the vista of old Regent Street with its stuccoed arcades. The prospect is now, however, destroyed by the ugly blank walls of Broadcasting House. After being damaged by bombing during the Second World War the church was restored and completely modernised internally in 1951.

Apsley House

See Wellington Museum

Bank of England   J3

Address
Threadneedle Street, EC2

Underground station
Bank

Opening times
Admission to banking hall
only on prior application

The "Old Lady of Threadneedle Street" is the national bank of the United Kingdom – guardian of the national currency, adviser to the government in financial matters and responsible for the amount of money in circulation, withdrawing old banknotes from circulation and issuing new ones. It also influences the level of interest rates, though in August 1981 it abandoned the practice of publishing a minimum lending rate (previously "bank rate").

The Bank of England was incorporated by royal charter in 1694 as a private company in order to finance the war against Louis XIV of France, and was brought under government control only in 1946. The majestic building which it occupies was designed by Sir John Soane; begun in 1788, it was completed in 1833. Between 1924 and 1939 it was radically rebuilt by Sir Herbert Baker, who preserved Soane's façade and Corinthian columns but erected a new seven-storey complex behind them. The statues above the main entrance are by Sir Charles Wheeler.

Visitors are admitted only to the banking hall, and then only by prior arrangement.

Bank of England

*Banqueting House   G4

The Banqueting House was part of the old Whitehall Palace,
and is now again in use for government receptions.

Whitehall Palace was originally (13th c.) the London seat of
the archbishops of York, and later the residence of the powerful
Cardinal Wolsey, in the reign of Henry VIII. After Wolsey's fall
in 1529 the palace was enlarged and became a royal residence.
Henry VIII was married to Anne Boleyn in Whitehall Palace in
1533, and died there in 1547. His daughter Elizabeth was taken
from Whitehall to be confined in the Tower, later returning in
triumph as queen. Charles I was beheaded outside the palace,
and Oliver Cromwell lived and died in it in 1658. After William
III transferred his private residence to Kensington Palace, the
old palace was destroyed by fire (1698), and only the
Banqueting House was spared by the flames.

The Banqueting House, designed by Inigo Jones in the
Palladian style, was completed in 1622, replacing an earlier
building of the time of Henry VIII which was burned down in
1619. Following recent restoration it has recovered all its
original splendour.

The staircase leads up to the Banqueting Hall, a double cube 34
m long, 17 m across and 17 m high (110×55×55 ft). This is
notable particularly for the nine allegorical ceiling paintings by
Rubens, assisted by Jordaens and other pupils (1635). The
central scene depicts the Apotheosis of Charles I; another
painting symbolises the Union of England and Scotland.
Rubens received a fee of £3000 and a knighthood for his work.

Address
Whitehall, SW1

Underground stations
Charing Cross, Westminster

Opening times
Tues.–Sat. and Easter
Monday 10 a.m.–5 p.m.,
Sun. 2–5 p.m.

Closed
Good Friday

Admission charge

The Banqueting House was the scene not only of banquets but of a number of historic events. A bust of Charles I on the staircase marks the position of the window through which he walked to the scaffold erected in front of the Banqueting House. In the Banqueting Hall Cromwell was invited by Parliament to accept the crown; and here, too, after the Restoration, Parliament swore loyalty to Charles II.

Barbican Centre for Arts and Conferences   J2

Address
Barbican, EC2

Underground stations
Barbican, St Paul's,
Moorgate

The new Barbican Centre is situated about 10 minutes' walk N of St Paul's Cathedral, between Aldersgate Street and Moorgate Street. The development, which took more than 10 years, comprises flats for more than 6000 people (including three tower-blocks about 120 m (394 ft) high) together with the integrated Barbican Centre for Arts and Conferences which was opened in March 1982. The outdoor attractions include a lake, lawns, fountains and terraces. The only pre-war building still standing is the restored St Giles' Church (originally built in 1390). Here also are the Guildhall School of Music and Drama, a girls' secondary school and the science faculty of the City University.

The chief attraction, however, is undoubtedly the arts and conference centre. The Barbican Hall (for concerts and conferences), which has 2026 seats and simultaneous translation equipment, is the permanent home of the London Symphony Orchestra; the Barbican Theatre with 1166 seats is the London headquarters of the Royal Shakespeare Company. In addition there are a studio theatre holding 200, art galleries for temporary exhibitions together with a courtyard for sculpture, a municipal lending library, rooms for seminars, three cinemas, two exhibition halls and a full range of catering facilities.

Bethnal Green Museum (officially the Museum of Childhood, Bethnal Green)

Address
Cambridge Heath Rd, E2 9EA

Underground station
Bethnal Green

British Rail station
Cambridge Heath

Opening times
Mon.–Thurs. and Sat. 10 a.m.
–6 p.m., Sun. 2.30–6 p.m.

Closed
1 Jan., 1st Mon. in May,
24–26 Dec.

Admission free

The Bethnal Green Museum, a branch of the Victoria and Albert Museum (see entry), was opened in 1872. Housed in an unusual Victorian building of iron, glass and brick, it contains the finest collection of toys in the country, a paradise for children and collectors alike.

All the exhibits are delightful – the Oriental toy soldiers, the European teddy bears, the many kinds of doll – but perhaps the most appealing items are the dolls' houses, the dolls' clothes (including a selection of 19th and 20th c. wedding dresses) and the board games. The museum also has a display of the locally produced Spitalfields silk and a collection of 19th c. decorative art.

Big Ben

See Houses of Parliament

Banqueting Hall ▶

British Museum G2

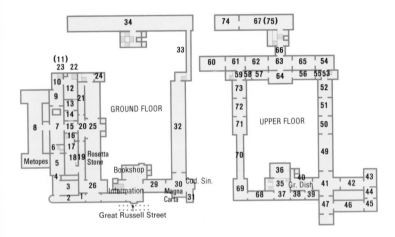

British Museum

GROUND FLOOR

1–2	Greek Bronze Age
3	Archaic Greece
4	Kouroi
5	Harpy Tomb
6	Bassae (mezzanine)
7	Nereid Monument
8	Sculptures from the Parthenon (Elgin Marbles)
9	Caryatids
10	Payava Tomb
11	Etruscan art (above 23)
12	Mausoleum (stairs down to 12A)
13	Hellenistic art
14–15	Roman art
16	Khorsabad
17	Assyria
18	Stair down to Assyrian Basement
19–20	Nimrud
21	Nineveh
22	Stair up to Greek and Roman architecture
23	Stair up to Etruscan art
24	Ancient Palestine
25	Egyptian sculpture
26	Assyrian Transept
29	Illuminated manuscripts
30	Historical, musical and literary manuscripts
31	Bible Room
32	King's Library
33	Maps
34	Art of Islam, S and SE Asia, China and Korea

UPPER FLOOR

35	Prehistoric and Roman Britain
36	Man before the Bronze and Iron Ages
37–39	Late prehistoric period in Europe
40	Roman Britain
41–42	Medieval art
43	Medieval pottery and tiles
44	Horological Room
45	Renaissance jewellery
46–47	Renaissance and later periods
49	Special exhibitions
50	Coins and medals
51	Ancient Persia (Persepolis)
52	Ancient Anatolia
53	Neo-Hittite sculpture
54	Sumerian and Babylonian goldsmiths' work (Ur)
55	Prehistoric Western Asia
56	History of writing
57	Ancient Syria
58	Ivories from Nimrud
59	South Arabia
60–61	Egyptian mummies
62	Egyptian tomb paintings and papyri
63	Everyday life in Eygpt
64	Egyptian pottery and small objects
65	Egyptian small sculpture
66	Coptic art
67	Prints and drawings
68	Greek, Etruscan and Roman bronzes and terracottas
69	Everyday life in ancient Greece and Rome
70	Greek mythology
71	Cypriot antiquities
72–73	Greek vases
74	Oriental painting
75	Japanese art (Lower Gallery)

The British Museum also houses the reference division of the British Library, originally the British Museum Library and still commonly known by that name.

Since 1757 the library has been a library of deposit: i.e. it receives a copy of every publication printed in Britain. Its nucleus was formed by the libraries of Sir Robert Cotton (d. 1631), Robert Harley, Earl of Oxford (d. 1724) and Sir Hans Sloane (d. 1753), together with the old Royal Library, presented by George II in 1757, and the library of George III, acquired in 1823. The Department of Printed Books contains more than 7 million volumes; the Department of Manuscripts more than 70,000 volumes and 10,000 manuscripts and papyri; the Department of Oriental Manuscripts and Printed Books more than 35,000 manuscripts and 250,000 printed books. It thus vies with the Bibliothèque Nationale in Paris for the status of the finest library in Europe. Its General Catalogue occupies 63 volumes, each of 500 pages.

The Museum itself has one of the finest collections in the world, covering the art and antiquities of Assyria and Babylonia, Egypt, Greece and Rome, Southern and South-East Asia and the European medieval period.

The British Museum, founded by Act of Parliament in 1753, was from 1759 accommodated in Montague House. The present neo-classical building was erected between 1823 and 1857. It was designed by Robert Smirke and completed by his brother Sydney, who was responsible for the circular Reading Room and the dome. The main front, 113 m (370 ft) long, has a colonnade of 44 Ionic columns. On the N side is the King Edward VII Building, erected in 1907–14.

Parts of the Museum are now housed in separate buildings, including the Museum of Mankind (6 Burlington Gardens, London W1) and the Natural History Museum (see entry).

The layout of the British Museum is shown in the plan on p. 38 (though the arrangement of the exhibits may be subject to change from time to time). With the help of this plan each

Address
Great Russell Street,
Bloomsbury, WC1

Underground stations
Russell Square, Holborn,
Tottenham Court Road

Opening times
Mon.–Sat. 10 a.m.–5 p.m.,
Sun. 2.30–6 p.m.

Closed
1 Jan., Good Friday, 1st
Mon. in May, 24–26 Dec.

Guided tours
Cassette guides
("Soundguides")

Admission free

British Museum: the Elgin Marbles

Reading Room of the British Library (British Museum)

visitor can locate exhibits of particular interest and plan a visit accordingly. Here only a few items of outstanding importance can be mentioned:

Sculpture from the Parthenon in Athens (Room 8), in particular the "Horse of Selene" from the E pediment. Of the four horses drawing the chariot of Selene, goddess of the moon, two are still in Athens; the fourth is lost.

In Room 25 stands the colossal bust of Ramesses II from the Ramesseum in Thebes-West; this room also houses the Rosetta Stone, a slab of black basalt with a trilingual inscription (in Egyptian hieroglyphic and demotic script and in Greek) dating from 195 B.C. which was found at Rosetta, in the Nile delta, in 1798 and enabled Champollion to decipher Egyptian hieroglyphics.

In Room 30 (Magna Charta Room) can be seen the Codex Sinaiticus (4th c.) and the Codex Alexandrinus (5th c.); these biblical manuscripts are among the most valuable of their kind in the possession of the museum.

The Mildenhall Treasure (Room 40), in particular the Great Dish, a large silver dish embossed with figures of Bacchus, Hercules and other mythological personages and with a bearded mask (probably the sea god Oceanus) surrounded by nymphs riding on sea monsters. The Mildenhall Treasure, a hoard of Roman silver dating from the 4th c. A.D., was found during ploughing operations at Mildenhall in Suffolk in 1942.

The Head of Aphrodite (Room 68), probably of the 4th c. B.C., found at Satala in Armenia. The head, which is double life-size, belonged to a torso; the left arm, holding a piece of material, was also found.

The Portland Vase (Room 69), formed of two layers of opaque glass: Roman work in the Greek style (2nd c. B.C.).

Brompton Oratory D4
(officially the London Oratory of St Philip Neri)

This Roman Catholic church in Italian Renaissance style was built between 1854 and 1884; the dome was added in 1896. It is served by secular priests of the Institute of the Oratory, founded in Rome by St Philip Neri in 1575 and introduced into England in 1847 by Cardinal Newman. There is a statue of Newman in the courtyard.

The interior is notable for the magnificence and great breadth of the nave (the third largest in England, exceeded only by Westminster Cathedral (see entry) and York Minster) and for its rich decoration. Particularly fine are the Carrara marble figures of Apostles (originally in Siena Cathedral) between the pilasters; the monumental Renaissance altar in the Lady Chapel, with an altarpiece from the Dominican church in Brescia; the altar in St Winifrid's Chapel, with an altarpiece from Maastricht Cathedral; the marble decoration of the chapels; and a number of mosaics.

The Oratory is noted for organ recitals (the organ has almost 4000 pipes) and for its fine choral performances. (Notice of recitals is given in the press.) Visitors interested in church music will find it well worth while to enquire whether there is a recital at the Oratory during their stay.

Address
Brompton Road, SW7

Underground station
South Kensington

Opening times
7 a.m.–9 p.m.

Buckingham Palace

Household Cavalry before Buckingham Palace

*Buckingham Palace   F4

Since Queen Victoria's accession (1837) Buckingham Palace has been the London residence of the royal family. Originally built in 1703 for the Duke of Buckingham, it was purchased by George III in 1762. In 1825 George IV commissioned John Nash, his court architect to alter and enlarge the palace; the E wing was added in 1846; and in 1913, when George V was king, the E front was given its present neo-classical aspect by Sir Aston Webb.

When the sovereign is in residence the royal standard flies over the palace night and day. Guard is mounted by units of the Guards Division in full uniform. On great occasions the sovereign appears, with members of the royal family, on the central balcony.

In front of the palace is the Queen Victoria Memorial, designed by Sir Aston Webb, with sculpture by Sir Thomas Brock.

A visit to Buckingham Palace should be timed to take in the colourful ceremony of the changing of the guard (daily, 11.30 a.m.) as well as a visit to the Queen's Gallery (Tues.–Sat. 11 a.m.–5 p.m., Sun. 2–5 p.m.), where there are varying displays of items from the extensive royal art collections.

Address
The Mall, SW1

Underground stations
St James's Park, Victoria, Hyde Park Corner, Green Park

Opening times
Not open to the public. Changing of the guard daily at 11.30 a.m. during the summer; every other day during the winter

The Queen's Gallery Opening times
Tues.–Sat. and Bank Holidays 11 a.m.–5 p.m., Sun. 2–5 p.m.

Burlington Arcade   F3

This very attractive and very expensive shopping arcade lies in the heart of the West End.

Address
Piccadilly, W1

Burlington Arcade

Underground stations
Piccadilly Circus, Green Park

Its character is indicated by the old regulations, which specified that the arcade was intended for the sale of haberdashery, clothing and other articles which offended neither sight nor smell, and prohibited whistling, singing, playing a musical instrument, carrying a parcel and putting up an umbrella within its precincts.

Burlington House

See Royal Academy

Cenotaph   G4

Situation
Whitehall, SW1

Underground station
Westminster

The Cenotaph, Britain's memorial to the dead of the two world wars, stands in Whitehall (see entry), in the heart of London's government and administrative quarter. Designed by Sir Edward Lutyens, it bears the simple inscription "To the Glorious Dead". The term cenotaph means "empty tomb". Originally constructed of plaster, it was rebuilt in Portland stone in deference to public feeling and unveiled on the second anniversary of the 1918 armistice, 11 November 1920. In the years after the First World War (the Great War) men raised their hats when passing the Cenotaph, even when they were on the top deck of a bus.

The Cenotaph bears no religious symbols, in recognition of the fact that the dead belonged to many different races and faiths, but only military emblems – the flags of the army, the air force, the navy and the merchant fleet.

Every year on Remembrance Day (the second Sunday in November) at 11 a.m. a memorial service in honour of those who died is held at the Cenotaph, in the presence of the Queen, Members of Parliament, members of the armed forces and other representatives of public life.

Charterhouse   H2

Charterhouse, originally a Carthusian priory, is now a home for poor gentlemen, who must be members of the Church of England, bachelors or widowers, over the age of 60 and retired officers or clergymen.

The original Charterhouse (from the French "Chartreuse") was founded in 1371 by Sir Walter de Manny, an officer in Edward III's army. After the dissolution of the priory in 1537 the property passed through various hands, including those of John Dudley, Duke of Northumberland (executed 1553) and Thomas Howard, Duke of Norfolk (executed 1572), and was finally purchased by Thomas Sutton, who then founded Charterhouse School. This developed into one of the country's leading public schools, which in 1872 moved to Godalming in Surrey.

The buildings, damaged in the Second World War, have since been carefully restored. All of them contain 16th and 17th c. work. Notable features are:

The Master's Court, which is entered by way of the Gatehouse (15th c., modernised). The stone walls on the E side of the court belong in part to the original monastic church.

The Chapel, originally the chapterhouse, which contains the founder's tomb. Also of interest are the chancel wall and the choir.

The Great Hall, on the N side of the Master's Court, which was built in the 16th c. with stone from the old monastic buildings. It is now the dining hall.

The Library (17th c.), adjoining the Great Hall.

The Great Chamber, in the Library; a magnificent room with a richly decorated stucco ceiling and old Flemish tapestries.

Address
Charterhouse Square, EC1

Underground station
Barbican

Opening times
April–July, Wed. at 2.45 p.m.

Admission charge

Chelsea Old Church   D5

Chelsea Old Church, on the Thames embankment, was founded in the 12th c., several times altered in later centuries, severely damaged by bombing during the Second World War and excellently restored in 1954–8.

The More Chapel was built by Sir Thomas More in 1528. Two Renaissance capitals on the arch leading into the original Italian chancel were probably designed by Holbein, who was a close friend of More's. In the Lawrence Chapel Henry VIII was secretly married to Jane Seymour a few days before the official marriage ceremony.

Address
All Saints, Cheyne Walk, Chelsea, SW3

Underground station
Sloane Square

Opening times
Mon.–Sat. 10 a.m.–noon and 2–4 p.m., Sun. 2–4 p.m.

Closed
Good Friday, Easter Day,
25 Dec.

Admission free

There are numerous 17th and 18th c. monuments, including that of Lady Jane Cheyne, by Bernini, on the N wall, and the tomb of the celebrated scientist, Sir Hans Sloane (d. 1753), in the SE corner of the churchyard.

*Chelsea Royal Hospital   E5

Address
Royal Hospital Road,
Chelsea, SW3

Underground station
Sloane Square

Opening times
Mon.–Sat. 10 a.m.–noon
and 2–4 p.m., Sun. 2–4 p.m.

Closed
Good Friday, Easter Day,
25 Dec.

Admission free

Chelsea Pensioners

Built 300 years ago as a home for veteran and invalid soldiers, the Royal Hospital still houses more than 500 "Chelsea pensioners", old and disabled soldiers who on special occasions wear the traditional uniform of Marlborough's time, with scarlet frock-coats in summer and dark blue overcoats in winter.

The Hospital was founded by Charles II in 1682, probably on the model of Louis XIV's Hôtel des Invalides in Paris (1670). The original buildings were designed by Wren (1682–92); an extension was built by Robert Adam (1765–82); and the complex was completed by Sir John Soane (1819).

The entrance to the Hospital is by the London Gate, on the NE. To the E of the road is a museum illustrating the history of the Royal Hospital.

In the Figure Court is a bronze statue of Charles II, a masterpiece by Grinling Gibbons. On Founder's Day (29 May) this is decked with oak boughs (commemorating Charles's escape after the Battle of Worcester by hiding in an oak-tree), and the pensioners receive double pay.

In the main building is the Great Hall, the finely panelled dining hall of the Hospital. On the walls are royal portraits and copies of flags captured from America and France. At the W end is an equestrian portrait of Charles II.

In the Governor's House is the Council Chamber, originally designed by Wren, with later alterations by Adam. On the walls are pictures by Sir Anthony van Dyck, Sir Peter Lely and Sir Godfrey Kneller.

The Chapel, also by Wren, has been preserved in its original state. In the apse is a fine painting of the Resurrection by Sebastiano Ricci (1710).

In the Royal Hospital gardens, which stretch down to the Thames embankment, are a number of cannon, some of them captured from the French at the Battle of Waterloo. Every year, the famous Chelsea Flower Show is held here.

Chelsea Town Hall   D5

Address
King's Road, Chelsea, SW1

Underground station
Sloane Square

Opening times
Not open to the public

Twice a year, in spring and autumn, the world-famous Chelsea Antiques Fair transforms the old town hall of Chelsea (built 1887) into a happy hunting ground for collectors. The setting is appropriate to the goods on display, which must be genuine antiques – i.e. furniture, carpets, china, glass, silver, jewellery, pictures and books dating from before 1830.

Clarence House

See St James's Palace

Cleopatra's Needle   G3

Although this obelisk of pink granite, standing 21 m (68 ft) high and weighing 180 tons, comes from Egypt, it has no connection with Cleopatra. It was presented to Britain by Mohammed Ali, Viceroy of Egypt, in 1819, but was brought to London (after a stormy voyage in which six seamen were lost) only in 1878. It was set up on the Victoria Embankment and was at once christened by Londoners with the nickname by which it is still known.

The obelisk is one of a pair (its companion being in Central Park, New York) erected at Heliopolis about 1500 B.C. The hieroglyphic inscriptions glorify the deeds and victories of Tuthmosis III and Ramesses II, the Great.

Situation
Victoria Embankment, WC2

Underground station
Embankment

Commonwealth Institute   B4

The modern building (1962) of the Commonwealth Institute, at the S end of Holland Park, houses displays by the Commonwealth countries illustrating their historical, socio-logical and artistic development. Separate sections are devoted to the landscape, minerals, way of life and economic progress of the various countries.

Attached to the Institute are an art gallery and a cinema in which there are daily shows of films from or about Commonwealth countries (Mon.–Fri. at 12.15, 1.15 and 4.25 p.m.; Sat. at 2.45, 3.30 and 4.25 p.m.; Sun. at 3, 3.30 and 4.40 p.m.).

The Commonwealth Institute is the successor to the old Imperial Institute, founded on the occasion of Queen Victoria's Golden Jubilee (1887) to promote a better understanding of the lands and peoples of the Commonwealth and Empire.

If you are contemplating a trip to one of the Commonwealth countries, it is worth remembering that the Institute's library (with a newspaper department) contains a wealth of information about the various countries, and that its infor-mation bureau can provide answers to any questions that arise in connection with your journey.

Address
Kensington High Street, W8

Underground station
High Street Kensington

Opening times
Mon.–Sat. 10 a.m.–
4.30 p.m., Sun. 2–5 p.m.

Closed
1 Jan., Good Friday, 1st
Mon. in May, 24–26 Dec.

Admission free

County Hall   G4

County Hall, a nine-storey building with more than 1500 rooms, occupying a $6\frac{1}{2}$-acre site on the S bank of the Thames at the end of Westminster Bridge, is the headquarters of the Greater London Council. The public are admitted to meetings of the Council, which are held in the Council Chamber on alternate Tuesdays at 2.30 p.m.

The building, in neo-Renaissance style, was begun in 1912 but not completed until 1932. New wings were added in 1936 and 1956.

There is a good view of County Hall, with its 229-m-long (750 ft) façade, centred on a semicircular colonnade, and its steeply

Address
Belvedere Road, South
Bank, SE1

Underground stations
Westminster, Waterloo

Opening times
alternate Tuesdays at
2.30 p.m. (except during
holidays)

Admission free

County Hall, home of the Greater London Council

pitched roof, from the Victoria Embankment on the opposite side of the Thames. There is a plan to lay out a riverside walk from County Hall to London Bridge (see entry), so that pedestrians will be able to follow the S bank of the Thames from Westminster to the City. The riverside terrace at County Hall, the first section of this project, affords a magnificent prospect of the Houses of Parliament (see entry) on the opposite bank, the view extending downstream to Waterloo Bridge and the National Theatre (see entry) on the S bank.

Courtauld Institute Galleries   F2

Address
Courtauld-Warburg Building, Woburn Square, WC1

Underground stations
Goodge Street, Russell Square, Euston Square

Opening times
Mon.–Sat. 10 a.m.–5 p.m., Sun. 2–5 p.m.

Closed
1 Jan., Good Friday, 24–26 Dec.

Admission charge

The Courtauld Institute Galleries house valuable art collections bequeathed to London University, in particular by Samuel Courtauld, Lord Lee of Fareham, and Roger Fry.

The Courtauld Collection is one of the finest collections of Impressionist and post-Impressionist pictures in Britain, with works by Manet, Degas, Monet, Renoir, Seurat, Gauguin and van Gogh. The Lee Collection contains works by Bartolomeo di Giovanni, Giovanni Bellini, Botticelli, Veronese, Bernardino Luini, Tintoretto, Goya, and Rubens, and portraits by British artists of the 17th–19th c. The Fry Collection, in addition to many works by the well-known art critic Roger Fry, consists of works by British and French artists of the late 19th and early 20th c.

Smaller bequests include works of sculpture, ivories and pictures.

Covent Garden

The Covent Garden quarter has taken on a fresh lease of life with the opening, in June 1980, of the new Covent Garden Market, billed as "London's new shopping experience". Here, only 15 minutes' walk from Piccadilly, is a remarkable concentration of delicatessen shops, fashion boutiques, craft stalls and specialised shops of all kinds. A new chapter has begun in the 300 years' history of the old flower and vegetable market of Covent Garden.

After the removal of the market to a more convenient site in 1974 a violent dispute arose between the municipal authorities, who wanted to pull down the old market hall, and the local people who were concerned to preserve the familiar aspect of the quarter and find other uses for the old market halls and warehouses.

The local people won, and Covent Garden has come to life again. One of the old warehouses is used for storing the properties of the Royal Opera House. In another an interesting antiques and junk market is held every Monday from 9 a.m. to 3.30 p.m. The new London Transport Museum has been opened here, and the Theatre Museum will be installed here when its new premises are ready. The main Market Building is now a specialised shopping centre, with shops and stalls open six days a week until 8 p.m., and a variety of restaurants.

And so this old quarter of London has taken on a new and modern aspect, for the benefit of both Londoners and visitors.

Underground station
Covent Garden

London Transport Museum

Opening times
10 a.m.–6 p.m. (last admission 5.15 p.m.)

Closed
25–26 December

Admission charge

Flea-market, Covent Garden

Crystal Palace Park and National Sports Centre

Situation
Penge, SE19

Underground station
Brixton

British Rail station
Crystal Palace

Distance
11 km (7 miles) S of central London

This public park with its children's zoo, ornamental ponds, boating lake and artificial ski-run is a popular resort for Londoners. Its principal attraction is the collection of lifesize plaster models of prehistoric animals – the only relic of the Great Exhibition of 1851 – on an island in the lake.

The Crystal Palace from which the park takes its name was the central feature of the Great Exhibition of 1851 – a masterpiece of cast-iron, steel and glass architecture designed by Sir Joseph Paxton – which was compared in its day to a waterfall suddenly petrified in mid-flow. It was brought here in 1854 from its original site in Hyde Park and was one of London's most notable landmarks until its destruction by fire in 1936. The site is now occupied by the National Sports Centre, run by the Greater London Council.

Downing Street   G4

Address
Whitehall, SW1

Underground stations
Embankment, Charing Cross

In this quiet, residential street the great decisions on British government policy are taken. No. 10 has been the official residence of the Prime Minister since 1732, when George II presented it to Sir Robert Walpole who, although he did not use the title, can be regarded as the first Prime Minister in the modern sense. No. 11 is the official residence of the Chancellor

10 Downing Street, residence of the Prime Minister

of the Exchequer, and No. 12 is the Government Whips' Office. All three houses are elegant Georgian buildings.

Downing Street was built by Sir George Downing, who contrived to hold office under both Cromwell and Charles II and was knighted by the latter in 1660.

*Dulwich College Picture Gallery

Barely 10 km (6 miles) S of central London is the residential district of Dulwich Village, which still preserves something of a village-like atmosphere, with its handsome Georgian villas, the only surviving London tollhouse, a park which in spring is gay with azaleas and rhododendrons, and the well-known Dulwich College.

The college was founded in the early 17th c. by Edward Alleyn (1566–1626), a wealthy Shakespearean actor and keeper of the King's wild beasts, as the College of God's Gift, and re-founded in the 19th c. as Dulwich College and Alleyn's School. The picture gallery, designed by Sir John Soane, was the first public art gallery in London (1814); it was restored after suffering severe damage during the Second World War.

The gallery contains works of various Dutch schools (Rembrandt, J. van Ruisdael, Aelbert Cuyp, etc.), 17th and 18th c. portraits by British painters (Sir Peter Lely, Sir Godfrey Kneller, William Hogarth, Thomas Gainsborough, Sir Joshua Reynolds, George Romney, Sir Thomas Lawrence), and pictures by Italian (Raphael, Paul Veronese, Guercino, Canaletto, Giovanni Battista Tiepolo, etc.), Flemish (Rubens, van Dyck, David Teniers), Spanish (Murillo, etc.) and French (Watteau, Poussin, Le Brun) masters.

Address
College Road, SE21

Underground station
Brixton

British Rail station
West Dulwich

Opening times
Tues.–Sat. 10 a.m.–1 p.m. and 2–5 p.m., Sun. 2–5 p.m.

Closed
1 Jan., Good Friday, 24–26 Dec.

Admission charge

Eton College

A visit to Windsor Castle (see entry) is usually combined with a visit to the little town of Eton with its world-famous public school. Eton lies across the Thames from Windsor at the N end of the Windsor Bridge, and the whole life of the town revolves around the school.

Eton College – officially the King's College of Our Lady of Eton – occupies a special place among the great English public schools. It was founded in 1440 by Henry VI. The pupils consist of "collegers", who have scholarships, and "oppidans", who pay the full fees and live in masters' houses. They wear the distinctive Eton school dress.

The main buildings, in red brick, are set around two quadrangles. The Upper School dates from 1689 to 1694, the Lower School from 1624 to 1639.

Particularly notable is the Chapel, in Perpendicular style, which was originally intended to be the choir of a much larger church. It contains a number of monuments and a series of very fine late 15th c. wall paintings (scenes from the life of the Virgin) which were painted over in the second half of the 16th c., rediscovered in the 19th c. and restored in 1928.

Address
Slough Road, Eton, Berks.

Telephone dialling code
075 35

Distance
35 km (22 miles) W of London on M4

Opening times
During term 2–5 p.m.; during holidays 10.30 a.m.–5 p.m.

Admission charge

In the gardens is a bronze statue of Henry VI (by Francis Bird, 1719). A gatehouse of 1520, Lupton's Tower, leads into the Cloisters, with the Hall (1450) and Library (1729).

Fleet Street   H3

Underground stations
Blackfriars, Temple (closed Sun.)

Fleet Street, the "street of ink", is the hub of the British newspaper world. In and around this street are the offices of the great national newspapers, the international news agencies and leading foreign newspapers.

Since the early days of Fleet Street as a home of the printed word – dating from the establishment of the first printing press here at the end of the 17th c. and the appearance of the first daily newspaper in 1702 – the newspaper industry has spread out far beyond the confines of this narrow street; but its core is still here, and Fleet Street has become a synonym for the whole of the British press.

Among its historic buildings are two 17th c. pubs, the Old Cheshire Cheese, once the resort of literary celebrities, and the Old Cock Tavern, the haunt of journalists and printers (see Practical Information, Pubs); the Church of St Dunstan in the West, which has a contemporary statue of Queen Elizabeth I on the S wall; and No. 1 Fleet Street, the house "at the sign of the marigold by Temple Bar", which housed Child's Bank, the oldest bank in London (founded 1671), which Dickens used as the model for Tellson's Bank in "A Tale of Two Cities".

Fleet Street, centre of the British newspaper world

Foundling Hospital Art Treasures

G2

The Foundling Hospital – now the Thomas Coram Foundation for Children – was established by Captain Thomas Coram in 1739 to care for abandoned children. William Hogarth painted a portrait of the founder and persuaded other artists to present pictures to the foundation in order to raise money for its charitable purposes. The gallery which was thus created became a rendezvous of the fashionable world in the time of George II.

In 1926 the hospital moved to Berkhamsted but the gallery remained in London. It contains pictures by Hogarth, Reynolds, Kneller, Gainsborough and Millais, a cartoon by Raphael, mementoes of Handel, who was a friend of Coram's, and various items connected with the history of the Foundling Hospital.

Address
40 Brunswick Square, WC1

Underground station
Russell Square

Opening times
Mon.–Fri. 10 a.m.–4 p.m.

Admission charge

*Geological Museum

D4

The Geological Museum has a very extensive and interesting collection of material on the geology and the minerals of the world. There are regular lectures and film shows on particular subjects.

In the Main Hall is a rotating globe 2 m (6 ft) in diameter, and the ground floor is devoted to the "Story of the Earth". The Museum has a famous collection of gem stones, showing the stones both in their natural state and after cutting and polishing. A special display illustrates the story of "Britain before Man", and other sections are concerned with the regional geology of Britain and with economic mineralogy. Specimens of rocks brought back from the moon by the spacecraft "Apollo" are also to be seen.

The Museum has a large library of some 70,000 books and 32,000 maps.

Address
Exhibition Road, South Kensington, SW7

Underground station
South Kensington

Opening times
Mon.–Sat. 10 a.m.–6 p.m.,
Sun. 2.30–6 p.m.

Closed
1 Jan., Good Friday, 1st Mon. in May, 24–26 Dec.

Admission free

Gray's Inn

G/H2

Gray's Inn is one of the four Inns of Court which have the exclusive right of admitting lawyers to practise as barristers in the English courts. The others are the Middle and Inner Temples, both housed in the Temple (see entry), and Lincoln's Inn (see entry).

Gray's Inn is said to have been in existence as early as the 14th c. (though this is the subject of dispute). It takes its name from the former owners of the site, the Lords de Gray. The buildings are set in beautiful gardens, which are open to the public from May to September. Children are not admitted.

To see the interesting Chapel, Hall and Library application should be made to the Undertreasurer. The 16th c. Hall has fine 16th and 17th c. heraldic windows with the coats of arms of Treasurers of the Inn. Shakespeare's "Comedy of Errors" was performed here for the first time in 1594.

In the Library is a statue of the philosopher and statesman Francis Bacon, the most notable member of the Inn, who lived here from 1576 to 1626.

Address
Gray's Inn Road, WC2

Underground station
Chancery Lane

Opening times
Gardens: May–July, Mon.–Fri. noon–2 p.m.; Aug.–Sept., Mon.–Fri. 9.30 a.m.–2 p.m.
Buildings: by prior arrangement

Closed
1 Jan., Good Friday, 24–26 Dec.

Admission free

* * Greenwich

Underground station
Surrey Docks

British Rail stations
Maze Hill, Greenwich

Thames launches
Westminster Pier to
Greenwich Pier

Greenwich, one of London's most attractive suburbs, lies 10 km (6 miles) downstream from London Bridge on the S bank of the Thames. It is famous for its Observatory (through which runs the Greenwich Meridian), its large Park, the National Maritime Museum and the old Greenwich Hospital which now houses the Royal Naval College. The most pleasant way to reach Greenwich is by river from Westminster Pier.

"Cutty Sark" and "Gipsy Moth IV"

Situation
Greenwich Pier

British Rail station
Greenwich

Thames launches
Greenwich Pier

Opening times
Mon.–Sat. 11 a.m.–6 p.m.,
Sun. 2.30–6 p.m. (in winter
to 5 p.m.)

The "Cutty Sark", now a museum ship, is the last of the old tea clippers which sailed between Britain and China in the 19th c. Built in 1869, it was the finest and, with its speed of 17 knots, the fastest sailing ship of its day. It was laid up here in 1956, and now contains an interesting collection of old ships' figureheads, prints and drawings, and mementoes of its voyages to China, India and Ceylon.

Close by is "Gipsy Moth IV", the yacht in which Sir Francis Chichester sailed singlehanded round the world.

Both ships are closed on Christmas Eve, Christmas Day and New Year's Day, but are open on Good Friday and Boxing Day (26 December). Children under 14 are admitted only if accompanied by an adult.

Greenwich Park

British Rail station
Maze Hill

Thames launches
Greenwich Pier

Greenwich Park was laid out as a royal park for Charles II to the design of Le Nôtre, Louis XIV's landscape gardener. It is now a pleasant public park, with tree-lined avenues, large flower borders, ponds and a bird sanctuary, together with tennis courts, a cricket ground, children's play areas and a restaurant.

National Maritime Museum and Queen's House

Address
Romney Road

British Rail station
Maze Hill

Opening times
Tues.–Sat. 10 a.m.–6 p.m.,
Sun. 2–5.30 p.m. (5 p.m. in
winter); open spring and
autumn bank holidays

Closed
1 Jan., Good Friday, 24, 25
Dec., Tues. following spring
and autumn bank holidays

Admission free

The National Maritime Museum, housed in the 17th c. Queen's House and in the two 19th c. wings which flank it, has a magnificent collection illustrating the history of the British navy and merchant shipping fleet from Tudor times to the present day. It begins in the Queen's House with the Tudor and Stuart periods (late 15th to early 18th c.), continues in the Caird Gallery with the period of the Napoleonic wars and ends in the East Wing with the naval history of the Second World War.

The Queen's House is a building of great interest in its own right. A Palladian mansion designed by Inigo Jones – imitated in many other houses of the period but never equalled – it is a masterpiece of classical architecture, notable for its symmetrical proportions, harmoniously contrived detail and finely executed marble floors, wrought-iron balustrades and carved and painted ceilings. The house, begun in 1617, was

The old tea clipper "Cutty Sark" ▶

commissioned by James I as a residence for his wife, Anne of Denmark, but was abandoned after Anne's death. Then in 1629 Charles I had it completed by Inigo Jones for his wife, Henrietta Maria. With Greenwich Park as its setting, it is a truly royal residence.

The East and West Wings, added in 1805–16, are linked with the Queen's House by colonnades. They were occupied by the Royal Hospital School for the children of sailors and marines until it moved to Suffolk in 1933. The museum was opened in 1937.

A room in the West Wing is devoted to relics of Nelson, including the uniform which he wore at the Battle of Trafalgar. Other interesting rooms are:

The Students' Room, containing thousands of prints, drawings and photographs.

The Barge House, where the state barges of Mary II (1689) and Frederick, Prince of Wales (1732) can be seen.

The Navigation Room, with Harrison's chronometer, the first timekeeper sufficiently accurate to be used for navigation.

The Neptune Hall, where displays illustrate the history of shipbuilding and there is a charming collection of figureheads. The pictures in the main galleries form a small art gallery in their own right. They include seascapes by Van de Velde, William Turner and Muirhead Bone, and portraits of famous seamen by leading artists (Kneller, Lely, Hogarth, Reynolds, Gainsborough, Romney).

Old Royal Observatory and Planetarium

Address
Flamsteed House,
Greenwich Park

British Rail station
Maze Hill

Thames launches
Greenwich Pier

Opening times
Tues.–Sat. 10 a.m.–6 p.m.,
Sun. 2–5.30 p.m. (in winter to 5 p.m.)

Closed
1 Jan., Good Friday, 25 Dec.

Admission free

The Royal Observatory, founded in 1675 by Charles II to promote safer navigation, was housed until 1957 in Flamsteed House, designed for the purpose by Sir Christopher Wren. On a mast topping one of its towers is a red ball which drops from the top of the pole at 1 o'clock precisely every day – a device originally intended to enable vessels in the river to regulate their chronometers. The Observatory is now at Herstmonceux in Sussex, while the Old Royal Observatory contains a collection of old astronomical instruments, including four chronometers dating from 1736 to 1764. Through it runs the Prime Meridian, which divides the globe into a western and an eastern half.

The Caird Planetarium was opened in 1965. Illustrated public lectures (admission charge) are given in the Planetarium during school holidays on Mondays, Tuesdays, Thursdays and Fridays, and also on certain Saturdays during the summer.

Royal Naval College

Address
King William Walk

Underground station
Surrey Docks

British Rail station
Maze Hill

No visit to Greenwich should omit the Painted Hall and Chapel of the old Greenwich Hospital, now the Royal Naval College. The College occupies a historic site, originally occupied by a palace erected by Edward I (1272–1307) and later by the Palace of Placentia built by the Duke of Gloucester in 1428, a favourite residence of Henry VII and other Tudor monarchs. Here Henry VIII was born, married Catherine of Aragon and Anne of Cleves, and signed the death warrant of Anne Boleyn.

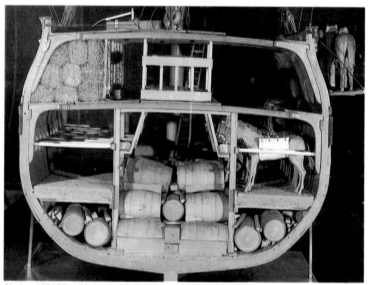

National Maritime Museum: section through the hull of a ship

Greenwich Observatory

Royal Naval College

Guildhall

Thames launches
Greenwich Pier

Opening times
Mon.–Wed. and Fri.–Sun.
2.30–5 p.m.

Closed
Public holidays

Admission free

His daughters Mary I and Elizabeth I were born in the palace, as was Edward VI. In the time of Cromwell it was used as a prison. In 1664 John Webb began to build a new palace for Charles II, and this was completed by Wren in 1696–8, by which time it had been decided to use the building as a home and hospital for disabled seamen.

The Painted Hall in the SW block (the King William Building) was completed by Wren in 1703. The ceiling paintings (by Sir James Thornhill, 1727) depict William III and Mary II.

The Chapel in the SE block (the Queen Mary Building), was also designed by Wren but completed by Ripley in 1752 and rebuilt after a fire by "Athenian" Stuart in 1789. It was restored in 1955.

Notable features of the Chapel are the altarpiece (St Paul's Shipwreck) by Benjamin West and the round pulpit, lectern and font, made of wood from the old dockyard at Deptford.

*Guildhall   J3

Address
King Street, Cheapside, EC2

Underground stations
Bank, Mansion House

Opening times
Mon.–Fri. 9.30 or 10 a.m.–
5 p.m.

The Guildhall, the administrative headquarters of the City of London and meeting-place of the Court of Common Council, dates from 1411, although the only surviving parts of the original building are sections of the external walls, the Great Hall and the crypt.

The porch, with the coat of arms of the City of London (motto "Domine dirige nos", "Guide us, O Lord"), leads into the Great Hall, which is over 46 m long, 15 m wide and 27 m high (150×

Old and new: the Guildhall

48×90 ft). In this hall the Court of Common Council meets every third Thursday at 1 p.m. to discuss municipal business.

Closed
1 Jan., Good Friday, 24–26 Dec.

Admission free

The public are admitted to these meetings, at which the city fathers appear in all their splendour, complete with the sceptre-bearer and sword-bearer, the recorder, chamberlain and other officers, and the chairman of the City's finance committee, still known as the Coal, Corn and Finance Committee. Other public occasions are the election of sheriffs on 24 June, a picturesque and colourful ceremony held on a dais erected at the E end of the Great Hall, and the swearing in of the new Lord Mayor, another annual ceremony conducted with traditional ritual.

(For admission to these meetings, or for information, apply to the Guildhall or to a tourist information office: see Practical Information.)

The Guildhall is also used for official receptions and banquets, and is closed to the public for three days before and four days after such occasions.

But the Great Hall is well worth seeing even on "ordinary" days. Its timber roof was destroyed in 1940 and rebuilt by Sir Giles Gilbert Scott with stone arches and a panelled ceiling.

Around the hall are banners bearing the arms of the 12 great "livery companies" (see General, Election of Lord Mayor), the old city guilds – the Skinners, Haberdashers, Ironmongers, Clothworkers, Vintners, Salters, Merchant Taylors, Goldsmiths, Drapers, Mercers, Grocers and Fishmongers. Their arms are also painted on the cornices. On the windows are inscribed the names of Lord Mayors.

Going towards the W end of the hall, we pass the Royal Fusiliers' Memorial and the only surviving 15th c. window. The W end is occupied by the gallery, with a minstrels' gallery above it; this end also has a fine oak screen and figures of Gog and Magog.

Along the N wall are statues of Sir Winston Churchill, Nelson, the Duke of Wellington, William Pitt the Younger and the Earl of Chatham (William Pitt the Elder). The two galleries are for peers and the Lady Mayoress.

The E end of the hall has fine oak panelling. On a dais are the seats occupied by members of the Court of Common Council.

Finally the visitor is shown the City sword and sceptre, housed in a canopied oak dresser.

Under the Great Hall is the 15th c. Crypt, which is also open to visitors. Restored after war damage, it has one of the finest medieval groined vaults in London.

To the E of the Great Hall is the Library, recently rehoused here. Anyone interested in the history of London should visit the Library. It has a unique collection of London prints and more than 140,000 volumes on the history of the city. Items of particular interest include a First Folio of Shakespeare, a map of London dated 1581 and a deed of purchase of a house bearing Shakespeare's signature. The library is open Mon.–Fri. from 9.30 a.m.–5 p.m.

Also of interest is the Guildhall Clock Museum, with 700 exhibits illustrating 500 years of clockmaking. The Museum is open Mon.–Fri. from 9.30 a.m.–5 p.m.

Ham House

Ham House

Address
Petersham, Surrey

Underground station
Richmond

Opening times
Apr.–Sept., Tues.–Sun.
2–6 p.m.; Oct.–Mar., noon–
4 p.m.

Closed
1 Jan., Good Friday, 1st
Mon. in May, 24–26 Dec.

Admission charge

Ham House, a National Trust property set in a large park near Richmond, is now an annexe of the Victoria and Albert Museum displaying 17th c. furniture and furnishings.

The original Ham House was a modest country house built by Sir Christopher Vavasour in 1610. In the middle of the 17th c. Elizabeth, Countess of Dysart, inherited it, and she, after her marriage to the Duke of Lauderdale, Charles II's favourite and minister, rebuilt and enlarged it in the lavish Baroque style of the period (1673–5). German, Dutch and Italian artists were employed in the decoration and embellishment of the interior, and Ham House soon came to be compared with a princely mansion.

It has been preserved largely in the condition in which the Lauderdales left it, and, with its beautiful grounds, is an impressive example of a sumptuous 17th c. country mansion.

** Hampton Court Palace

British Rail station
Hampton Court

Thames launches
Hampton Court Bridge

Hampton Court Palace, perhaps the finest and most interesting of Britain's royal palaces, lies SW of London on the N bank of the Thames. It is no longer a royal residence, but part of the palace is still occupied by persons who have been granted "grace and favour" apartments by the monarch.

The palace was built between 1514 and 1520 as a private residence for Cardinal Wolsey, who presented it to Henry VIII in order to secure the king's favour. The Great Hall and other parts of the palace date from Henry's occupation. Five of his six wives (the exception being Catherine of Aragon) lived here as queen, and the ghosts of his third and fifth wives, Jane Seymour and Catherine Howard, are said to haunt the palace. It was a favourite residence of Elizabeth I, who heard of the defeat of the Spanish Armada while staying here. Charles I also lived at Hampton Court, both as king and as Cromwell's prisoner.

The first major alterations to the palace were carried out in the reign of William and Mary, when the E wing was rebuilt by Wren in Renaissance style, the Tudor W part remaining unaltered. The palace was opened to the public in the time of Victoria.

The main features of interest in the palace itself are the Clock Court, with its astronomical clock, made for Henry VIII in 1540; the State Apartments, including the Haunted Gallery; the Chapel; the Great Hall, with its magnificent hammerbeam roof and fine tapestries; the kitchens and cellars, which give some idea of the problems of provisioning a palace of this size; and the Tudor tennis court, which is still in use.

(The kitchens, cellars and tennis court are open only from April to September.) ·

Visitors should also take time to explore the grounds of the palace – the Privy Garden, the Pond Garden, the Elizabethan Knot Garden, the Broad Walk, the Wilderness. The gardens are at their best in mid-May, when the flowers are in full bloom.

Distance
25 km (15 miles) SW of London

Opening times
Park: daily
Palace: May–Sept., Mon.–Sat. 9.30 a.m.–6 p.m., Sun. 11 a.m.–6 p.m.
Nov.–Feb., Mon.–Sat. 9.30 a.m.–4 p.m., Sun. 2–4 p.m.; Mar., Apr., Oct., Mon.–Sat. 9.30 a.m.–5 p.m., Sun 2–5 p.m.

Closed
1 Jan., Good Friday, 24–26 Dec.

Admission charge

Hampton Court Palace

Also in the grounds are the Upper Orangery (open Apr.–Sept.) and the Lower Orangery (open throughout the year), which contains Mantegna's masterpiece, "The Triumph of Caesar". Both orangeries are open at the same times as the palace.

Another great attraction, particularly for children, is the famous Maze (open May–Sept., Mon.–Sat. 10 a.m.–6 p.m., Sun. 11 a.m.–6 p.m.; Oct., Mar. and Apr., Mon.–Sat. 10 a.m.–5 p.m., Sun. 11 a.m.–5 p.m.; closed Nov.–Feb.).

*Hayward Gallery   H3

Address
South Bank, SE1

Underground stations
Embankment, Waterloo

Opening times
Mon.–Thurs. 10 a.m.–8 p.m.,
Fri.–Sat. 10 a.m.–6 p.m.,
Sun. noon–6 p.m.

Closed
1 Jan., Good Friday, 25 Dec.
and between exhibitions

Admission charge

The Hayward Gallery, part of the new South Bank arts complex, is built in a style which aptly reflects its role as a gallery of modern art. Opened in 1968, the gallery is laid out on two levels, with intricate lighting installations to enable the pictures and objects to be seen at their best; the design of the interior, with rooms of widely varying size and height, also helps to achieve this objective. The layout can be varied by the use of movable partitions, and three open courts provide effective display areas for sculpture.

The gallery is mainly used by the Arts Council for the display of loan exhibitions.

The development of the South Bank as a centre of the arts, which was initiated by the old London County Council, has given this area an important place in the artistic life of the capital. Here, in addition to the Hayward Gallery, are the Royal Festival Hall (see entry), the Queen Elizabeth Hall and Purcell Room (See Practical Information, Music), the National Film Theatre, with three cinemas, and the National Theatre (see entry), with three separate auditoriums.

Horse Guards   G4

Address
Whitehall, SW1

Underground stations
Embankment, Charing Cross

Changing of the Guard
Mon.–Sat. at 11 a.m., Sun. at
10 a.m.; inspection at 4 p.m.

The Horse Guards, a finely proportioned building with a handsome clock tower designed by William Kent (1753), occupies the site of a guard house belonging to the old Palace of Whitehall. It is now occupied by military offices.

The Household Cavalry consists of two separate regiments, the Life Guards, who wear scarlet tunics and white plumed helmets, and the Blues and Royals, who wear blue tunics and red plumed helmets. The Life Guards originated as a cavalry unit which formed Charles I's bodyguard during the Civil War, the Blues and Royals (formerly the Royal Horse Guards) as a troop of Cromwellian cavalry.

The changing of the guard, which takes place at 11 a.m. on weekdays and 10 a.m. on Sundays, is one of London's prime tourist attractions.

The headquarters of the Household Cavalry are in Knights-bridge Barracks, facing on to Hyde Park. The daily 2-km ride (1½ miles) by the new guard from the barracks to the Horse Guards passes Buckingham Palace (see entry).

In June every year, on the Queen's official birthday, the parade ground behind the Horse Guards is the scene of a colourful military spectacle, Trooping the Colour.

Horse Guards

The Household Cavalry (Blues and Royals)

Houses of Parliament G4

Address
Parliament Square, SW1

Underground station
Westminster

Closed to visitors except for
those attending debates

The Houses of Parliament are officially known as the Palace of Westminster, recalling the fact that they occupy the site of a former royal palace, originally built by Edward the Confessor and enlarged by William the Conqueror and William Rufus. Westminster Hall was built by William Rufus.

The whole palace was destroyed by a catastrophic fire in 1512, with the exception of Westminster Hall, the 14th c. St Stephen's Chapel and the Crypt.

Until 1529, when Henry VIII acquired the neighbouring Whitehall Palace, the Palace of Westminster was a royal residence. In 1547 it became the seat of Parliament, the House of Commons meeting in St Stephen's Chapel and the House of Lords in a hall at the S end of Old Palace Yard (see General, Parliament).

In 1605 a group of Roman Catholics led by Guy Fawkes tried to blow up the Houses of Parliament; and to this day, before the state opening of Parliament, the vaults are searched by Yeomen of the Guard in their traditional uniform.

The present Houses of Parliament – in neo-Gothic style to harmonise with the nearby Westminster Abbey – were built between 1840 and 1888 to the design of Sir Charles Barry. They were officially opened in 1852. After the Second World War the House of Commons and other parts of the buildings were rebuilt in the original style.

(1) The Royal Entrance, a doorway 15 m (50 ft) high, is used by the monarch at the annual state opening of the Parliamentary session, usually in November.

(2) Entrance for visitors.

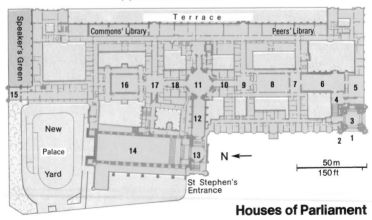

Houses of Parliament

1 Royal Entrance	7 Prince's Chamber	13 St Stephen's Porch
2 Visitors' Entrance	8 House of Lords	14 Westminster Hall
3 Victoria Tower	9 Peers' Lobby	15 Clock Tower (Big Ben)
4 Norman Porch	10 Peers' Corridor	16 House of Commons
5 Robing Room	11 Central Lobby	17 Commons' Lobby
6 Royal Gallery	12 St Stephen's Hall	18 Commons' Corridor

(3) The Victoria Tower, built 1858, is the largest and tallest square tower in the world (23 m (75 ft) square, 102 m (336 ft) high). When Parliament is sitting, the Union Jack flies from the top of the tower.

(4) The Royal Staircase leads to the Norman Porch, with statues and frescoes of the Norman period.

(5) Adjoining is the Robing Room, used by the monarch, 16 m (54 ft) long, decorated in the style of the early Victorian period. Notable features are the wall frescoes, the carved oak panels, with the badges of successive sovereigns, the fireplace made of a variety of marbles and a chair of state of the Victorian period.

(6) The Royal Gallery, 34 m (110 ft) long, has an elaborate ceiling and a frieze with the arms of English and Scottish monarchs. On the walls are two monumental frescoes by Daniel Maclise, "The Death of Nelson" and "The Meeting of Wellington and Blücher after Waterloo".

(7) The adjoining Prince's Chamber is the anteroom to the House of Lords. On the panelled walls are portraits of the Tudor monarchs and members of their families, and below these are bas-reliefs of scenes from their reigns. Opposite the entrance is a white marble statue of Queen Victoria, flanked by figures of Justice and Mercy.

(8) The House of Lords is a sumptuously decorated chamber, with red leather benches for the peers, the traditional "Woolsack" (recalling the importance of the English wool trade from the 14th c. onwards) on which the Lord Chancellor sits, and the throne occupied by the monarch when opening Parliament. Above the throne are galleries for distinguished visitors, above the N entrance the galleries for the press and the public.

In the recesses behind the galleries are frescoes depicting scenes from British history (S end) and symbolising Justice, Religion and Chivalry (N end). In the window niches are statues of the barons who compelled King John to sign Magna Carta in 1215.

The sittings of the House of Lords are public. Visitors are admitted at the St Stephen's Entrance and obtain a permit for admission at the Admission Order Office in St Stephen's Hall. Admission from 2.30 p.m. Mon.–Wed., 3 p.m. Thurs., 11 a.m. Fri.

(9) The Peers' Lobby, beyond the House of Lords, is a square chamber with a fine pavement of encaustic tiles.

(10) The Peers' Corridor leads into the Central Lobby.

(11) The Central Lobby, lying half-way between the Lords and Commons, is an elaborately decorated octagonal vestibule with a vaulted ceiling 23 m (75 ft) high.

(12) The door on the W side of the Central Lobby leads into St Stephen's Hall, on the site of the old St Stephen's Chapel, in which the House of Commons met from 1547 to 1834. This is a vaulted hall, 29 m (95 ft) long, with mosaics depicting the founding of the chapel by King Stephen. It contains statues of Norman and Plantagenet kings and queens and British statesmen of the 17th–19th c.

(13) From St Stephen's Porch, adjoining on the W, there is a view of Westminster Hall.

(14) Westminster Hall was spared by the fire which destroyed the old Palace of Westminster. Its most impressive feature is the

Houses of Parliament, with the Victoria Tower and Big Ben ▶

The Queen drives to the State Opening of Parliament

oak hammerbeam roof (late 14th c.), restored after damage during the last war.

Westminster Hall has been the scene of great historical events. From 1224 to 1882 it was the meeting-place of the highest courts in the land and witnessed many famous trials, including those of Richard II (1399), Sir Thomas More (1535) and Charles I (1649). Here, too, Cromwell was installed as Lord Protector in 1653.

From Westminster Hall a staircase leads down to St Stephen's Crypt (officially the church of St Mary Undercroft), the crypt of the old St Stephen's Chapel (1327).

(15) At the N end of the Houses of Parliament is the Clock Tower, which ranks with Trafalgar Square and Tower Bridge (see entries) as one of the most celebrated London landmarks. The tower is 98 m (320 ft) high, with a flight of 334 steps leading up to the clock, named Big Ben, which has dials 7 m (23 ft) in diameter and minute hands 4 m (14 ft) long. The bell which strikes the hours weighs 13 tons. The sound of Big Ben has become known throughout the world as the time signal of BBC radio.

(16) The House of Commons was destroyed by bombing during the last war but was rebuilt in its original form in order to retain the familiar atmosphere of the House. Even the original decoration was reproduced.

At the N end of the chamber is the chair, of black Australian wood, occupied by the Speaker, who presides over the House of Commons. The Speaker is so called because it was originally his responsibility to speak to the monarch and to represent to him the views of the House of Commons – a responsibility which could at times be hazardous (see General, Parliament). To this day a newly elected Speaker is expected to put on a show of reluctance when he is conducted to his chair for the first time.

The members of the government and opposition parties sit opposite one another on parallel rows of green benches. Between them is the table of the House, on which the mace is placed during sittings of the Commons. On the carpet between the front benches are two red lines, traditionally said to be two sword-lengths apart, which were originally designed to prevent members coming to blows.

The public are admitted to watch the proceedings of the House from the Strangers' Gallery. Visitors enter by the St Stephen's Entrance (queuing necessary before a major debate), obtain an admission order from the Admission Order Office in St Stephen's Hall (Mon.–Thurs. from 4.15 p.m., Fri. from 10 a.m.) and wait there to be conducted to the Strangers' Gallery by a liveried attendant.

At the opening of each day's sitting of the House of Commons the cry is heard: "Mr Speaker! Hats off – strangers!" This marks the passing of the Speaker's procession – the Speaker himself, wearing a wig and long black gown, preceded by a messenger and the Serjeant at Arms, wearing kneebreeches and carrying the mace, and followed by his train-bearer, chaplain and secretary. The proceedings begin with a prayer read by the chaplain, after which the public are admitted. Visitors are shown to their places in the gallery by frock-coated attendants wearing a large gold badge, who give them a copy of the order paper listing the day's business.

(17) The anteroom to the House of Commons is the Commons' Lobby, a square chamber in Gothic style with statues of 20th c. statesmen (including bronze figures of Sir Winston Churchill and Lloyd George).

(18) The Commons' Corridor leads back from here to the Central Lobby.

Hyde Park   D/E3/4

Hyde Park, together with Kensington Gardens, which adjoin it on the W, forms the largest open space in London, extending for 2 km (1¼ miles) from E to W and 1 km (½ mile) from N to S. Originally belonging to Westminster Abbey (see entry), it was taken over by Henry VIII in 1536 and became a royal deer-park. Charles I threw it open to the public in 1635. In 1730 Queen Caroline, George II's wife, laid out the Serpentine, an artificial lake which now offers Londoners facilities for rowing, sailing, swimming or merely watching the birds.

Underground stations
Hyde Park Corner, Marble Arch, Lancaster Gate

To the N of the Serpentine is a bird sanctuary, with Epstein's figure of "Rima", the bird-girl heroine of W. H. Hudson's novel, "Green Mansions". On the S side are a restaurant and bathing lido.

The main entrance to the park, at Hyde Park Corner (see entry), is a triple archway by Decimus Burton (1828), with a reproduction of the Parthenon frieze (see British Museum). Near this is a statue of Achilles (by Westmacott, 1822) cast from captured French cannon, erected in honour of the Duke of

Wellington. The statue is copied from a figure on the Quirinal in Rome. Nearby is a bandstand, where bands play on Sundays in summer.

From Hyde Park Corner (see entry) three roads run through the park. The Carriage Road, to the left, leads to the Albert Memorial (see entry); the East Carriage Road, to the right, leads to Marble Arch (see entry) and Speakers' Corner; and the one in the middle runs W to the Serpentine. Between them is Rotten Row (probably a corruption of the French "Route du Roi"), a horse-riding track almost 2 km (1 mile) long.

Hyde Park Corner   E4

Underground station
Hyde Park Corner

At Hyde Park Corner stands the Wellington Arch, a monumental triumphal arch commemorating Wellington's victory at Waterloo; it is surmounted by a bronze quadriga (four-horse chariot) with a figure of Peace.

Facing the Duke's residence, Apsley House (see Wellington Museum), is a bronze equestrian statue of Wellington; at the corners of the pedestal are figures of a Grenadier Guard, a Scottish Highlander, a Welch Fusilier and an Inniskilling Dragoon.

There are two other war memorials at Hyde Park Corner – the Royal Artillery War Memorial (1928) and the Machine Gun Corps War Memorial (1927), with a figure of David.

*Imperial War Museum   H4

Address
Lambeth Road, SE1

Underground stations
Lambeth North, Elephant and Castle

Opening times
Mon.–Sat. 10 a.m.–5.50 p.m., Sun. 2–5.50 p.m.

Closed
1 Jan., Good Friday, 1st Mon. in May, 24–26 Dec.

Admission free

The Imperial War Museum, covering the history of the two world wars, was founded in 1920 and moved to its present premises in the Geraldine Mary Harmsworth Park, Lambeth, in 1936.

The Naval Warfare Gallery includes among its exhibits a German one-man submarine, an Italian one-man torpedo, German magnetic mines, models of warships and submarines, and naval uniforms.

The Land Warfare Gallery, houses a historical section on "The Road to War" (1870–1914) and displays mortars, field and anti-aircraft guns, machine-guns, British and Indian uniforms, pioneers' and paratroopers' equipment.

The Air Warfare Gallery illustrates the development of military aircraft since 1914.

Jewel Tower (Houses of Parliament)   G4

Address
Old Palace Yard, SW1

Underground station
Westminster

The Jewel Tower, now a museum, is one of the few surviving remnants of the medieval Palace of Westminster (see Houses of Parliament), the royal residence from the time of Edward the Confessor (1003–66) to that of Henry VIII (1491–1547).

It was built by Henry Yevele in 1366 as a repository for the king's private wealth (as distinct from the Crown Jewels and the public treasury), and was used for that purpose until the death of Henry VIII. From the beginning of the 17th c. it was used to store the records of the House of Lords, and from 1869 to 1938 it was occupied by the Weights and Measures Department of the Board of Trade. Severely damaged during the Second World War, it was rebuilt in its original style between 1948 and 1956. The small vaulted rooms are now used for the display of relics of the old palaces of Westminster and Whitehall.

Opening times
Mon.–Sat. 10.30 a.m.–4 p.m.

Closed
Good Friday, Christmas, New Year's Day

Admission charge

*Kensington Palace   C4

Kensington Palace, the private residence of the monarch from 1689 to 1760, is now in part open to the public. Much of it is still occupied by members of the royal family and pensioners of the Crown occupying "grace and favour" apartments.

The original house was purchased by William III, who commissioned Wren to convert it into a royal residence, and the rebuilding was completed by William Kent in the reign of George I. The last king to reside in the palace was George II. Queen Victoria was born in Kensington Palace and received the news of her accession here, and Queen Mary, grandmother of the present Queen, was also born here. William III and Mary II, Queen Anne and George II died in the palace.

Visitors see the following rooms:

The State Apartments on the first floor (entrance at the NE corner of the palace), with pictures, mainly of the 17th and 18th c.

Address
Kensington Palace Gardens, W8

Underground stations
Queensway, High Street Kensington

Opening times
Mon.–Sat. 9 a.m.–5 p.m., Sun. 1–5 p.m.

Kensington Gardens

Kensington Palace

The Queen's Staircase (designed by Wren, 1690).

The Queen's Gallery, with oak panelling and royal portraits.

The Queen's Dining Room, Drawing Room, Closet and Bedroom, used by Queens Victoria, Mary and Anne, with their furniture.

The Cupola Room, with fine ceiling paintings and a clock, made in 1730, which is known as the "Temple of the Four Monarchies" (Assyria, Persia, Greece, Rome).

Various rooms occupied by Kings William III, George I and George II.

King William's Gallery (by Wren, 1694), 29 m (96 ft) long, with interesting paintings of 18th and 19th c. London, a ceiling painting ("Adventures of Ulysses") by Kent and woodcarving by Grinling Gibbons.

The Orangery (1704), recently redecorated. Although attributed to Wren, it is probably by Hawksmoor.

Outside the S front of the palace is a statue of William III, presented to Edward VII by William II of Germany. On the E side is a statue of Queen Victoria.

A visit to the palace should be combined with a stroll in Kensington Gardens, once the private gardens of the palace. Laid out in their present form in 1728–31 by Queen Caroline, they include such attractive features as the Sunken Garden, the Flower Walk and the Fountains. As in other royal parks, there are open-air concerts on Sundays in summer. There is also a pleasant open-air restaurant.

On the S side of Kensington Gardens is the Albert Memorial (see entry).

Kensington Palace

*Kew Gardens

Kew Gardens, officially the Royal Botanic Gardens, are situated in SW London on the S bank of the Thames. Here some 30,000 plants are identified every year, more than 45,000 plants are grown and specimens and information are exchanged with botanists and botanical institutions all over the world. Here, too, the Brazilian rubber tree was adapted to the climatic conditions of the Malay peninsula, and here was developed the Marquis strain of wheat which made it possible to bring the prairies of NW Canada into cultivation. The Herbarium contains a collection of over 7,000,000 dried plants and the Library has more than 50,000 volumes of botanical literature.

Notable features of Kew — apart from the sheer numbers of plants grown in this area of over 101 ha (250 acres) — are the historical herb garden behind Kew Palace and the jungle plants and palms in the huge glass-houses. (Open daily from 11 a.m.–4.50 p.m.; an hour longer in summer. Closed on 1 Jan. and 25 Dec.)

The gardens were first laid out in 1759 on the initiative of Princess Augusta, mother of George III. In 1841 they became government property, and in 1897 Queen Victoria added Queen's Cottage and the adjoining woodland. The little Kew Palace, officially known as the Dutch House, is open to the public (11 a.m.–5.30 p.m. daily from mid Mar.–mid Oct. except 1st Mon. in May). The palace was occupied by George III during his fits of madness, and Queen Charlotte, his wife, died here. The furniture, furnishings and pictures give a picture of the domestic life of the royal family in Georgian times.

The Queen's Cottage, built for Queen Charlotte in 1772 and recently restored in the original style, was a favourite residence of Queen Victoria. It stands in a garden which by Victoria's desire was left in its natural state as an area of woodland. (Open 11 a.m.–5.30 p.m. on Sat. and Sun. from Apr. to mid Oct.)

Other charming buildings in Kew Gardens are the Chinese pagoda (by Sir William Chambers, 1761) and the Japanese gateway, a copy of a gate in the Nishi-Honganji temple in Kyoto.

Address
Kew Road, Kew, Surrey

Underground station
Kew Gardens

British Rail station
Kew Bridge

Thames launches
Kew

Opening times
Summer daily 10 a.m.–7 or 8 p.m. winter 10 a.m.–4 p.m.

Closed
1 Jan., 1st Mon. in May, 25 Dec.

Admission charge

The Pagoda, Kew Gardens

*Lambeth Palace G4

Lambeth Palace, situated in beautiful grounds (the Archbishop's Park) at the E end of Lambeth Bridge, has been for more than 700 years the London residence of the Archbishop of Canterbury. Originally built at the end of the 12th c., the palace has preserved its medieval character in spite of later rebuilding and alteration and, more recently, bomb damage and subsequent restoration. Every ten years (most recently in 1978) the Lambeth Conference of Anglican bishops is held in the Great Hall of the palace.

Address
Lambeth Road, SE1

Underground station
Westminster

Lancaster House

See St James's Palace

Lambeth Palace

Leicester Square   G3

Underground station
Leicester Square

Leicester Square, long famous as a centre of entertainment, is built around a small garden laid out by Albert Grant in 1874. In the centre of the garden is a statue of Shakespeare, and at the corners are busts of four famous local residents – Sir Isaac Newton, Sir Joshua Reynolds, William Hogarth and Dr John Hunter. There is also a statue of Charlie Chaplin. The square is named after Leicester House, built here by the second Earl of Leicester in 1631. The N and S sides of the square have recently been made a pedestrian precinct. Around the square and in the immediately surrounding area are some of London's largest and best known cinemas.

*Lincoln's Inn   G/H3

Address
Chancery Lane, WC2

Underground station
Chancery Lane, Holborn

Opening times
Garden. Mon.–Fri.
9.30 a.m.–5 p.m. Chapel –
opened by gatekeeper

Lincoln's Inn is one of the four great Inns of Court (see Temple), the others being the Middle and Inner Temple and Gray's Inn (see entry). It is named after a 14th c. Earl of Lincoln who founded a school for the training of lawyers, and first appears in the records under its present name in 1422. Celebrated members of Lincoln's Inn have included Sir Thomas More, William Pitt, Horace Walpole, John Henry Newman, George Canning, Benjamin Disraeli, William Ewart Gladstone and H. H. Asquith.

Lincoln's Inn

The complex includes buildings dating from the 15th c. onwards, the 19th c. Library and New Hall (dining hall), the Chapel and numerous barristers' and solicitors' chambers, as well as the large and beautifully kept gardens.

The gardens and the Chapel are open to the public. The Chapel, originally built by Inigo Jones in Gothic style (1623), was radically restored by Wren in 1685. Notable features are the old oak pews, the 17th c. Flemish stained glass (restored) and the 18th c. pulpit. The open crypt below was for many years the meeting-place of barristers and their clients.

To see the halls and Library it is necessary to obtain written permission from the Treasurer of the Inn. The New Hall (1859) has a huge mural, 15 m (45 ft) high, by G. F. Watts. In the same building is the Library (founded 1497), which has a collection of over 80,000 law books.

Other elements in the complex are the Stone Buildings (18th c.), dwelling houses occupied by barristers; the 17th c. New Square, with barristers' chambers; the picturesque Old Buildings (16th and 17th c.); and the Old Hall (built 1491, restored 1924–8), which was occupied until 1883 by the Court of Chancery.

Closed
1 Jan., Good Friday to Easter Monday, 24–26 Dec.

Admission free

Lombard Street   J3

Lombard Street (named after the moneylenders from Lombardy who had their houses here in the 13th c.) has been London's banking and financial centre since medieval times.

Underground station
Bank

Lombard Street

Bank signs in Lombard Street

London Bridge

The street is of interest not so much for its 19th and 20th c. buildings, as for the bank signs hanging above the pavement – continuing a tradition dating from the Middle Ages, when illiteracy was rife and the bankers' customers were able to identify them only by their heraldic emblems.

London Bridge   J3

"London Bridge is falling down," says the old rhyme. In fact London Bridge has never fallen down, though it has twice been pulled down and replaced by a new bridge.

The London Bridge of the rhyme was a 12th c. stone bridge lined on both sides with houses, which were later removed to make room for recesses in which pedestrians could take refuge from the heavy traffic on the narrow carriageway. In 1831 this bridge was replaced by a new one, which by the 1960s had become inadequate to cope with the flow of traffic and was due in turn to be superseded by a more modern bridge. The 1831 bridge was then bought by an American (under the belief, it was said, that he was acquiring Tower Bridge), transported across the Atlantic and re-erected at Lake Havasu City in Arizona.

The present London Bridge was opened to traffic in 1973.

Address
King William Street, EC3

Underground station
Monument

London Dungeon   J3

The London Dungeon, British Tourist Authority award winner, is a gruesome display of the horrors of life in Britain from the Middle Ages to the 17th c. – the murder of Thomas Becket, the Plague, the burning of martyrs at the stake and scenes of torture – all with notices detailing the historical background.

There are also curious and interesting displays illustrating life in the Middle Ages – food and drink, diseases, witchcraft and astrology.

Address
Tooley street, SE1

Underground station
London Bridge

Opening times
Summer 10 a.m.–5.45 p.m., winter 10 a.m.–4.30 p.m.

Admission charge

*Madame Tussaud's   E2

Madame Tussaud's famous waxworks exhibition was originally established in Paris in 1770, moved to London in 1802 and transferred to its present site in 1835. The collection of figures of the famous and infamous of the past and present is kept constantly up to date, and in 1979 a new Chamber of Horrors was opened to satisfy the public appetite for ever more gruesome exhibits and displays.

Here the visitor will encounter Henry VIII and his six wives, the present Queen (who, like most of the contemporary figures represented here, gave special sittings to the waxwork artists) and royal family, leading figures of the French Revolution such as Robespierre and Marat (modelled from their severed heads by Madame Tussaud immediately after their execution), 20th c. statesmen including Churchill and Gandhi (recently also Mrs Thatcher), television and sporting personalities. Jack the

Address
Marylebone Street, NW1

Underground station
Baker Street

Opening times
10 a.m.–5.30 p.m.
(July, Aug. 10 a.m.–6 p.m.)

Closed
25 Dec.

Admission charge

Madame Tussaud's: Henry VIII and his six wives

Ripper and other notorious criminals have their place in the Chamber of Horrors. The battle of Trafalgar is re-fought in a striking tableau, and Nelson dies on the 'Victory'' amid the thunder and smoke of cannon.

Adjoining Madame Tussaud's is the London Planetarium, in which spectacular representations of the stars and planets are projected in a huge copper dome, with explanatory commentary.

Mansion House   J3

Address
Mansion House Street, EC4

Underground stations
Bank, Mansion House

Opening times
Tues.–Thurs., on written application only

The Mansion House, the official residence of the Lord Mayor, was built by George Dance the Elder between 1739 and 1753 but has undergone a number of later alterations. The imposing Corinthian colonnade serves a ceremonial as well as a decorative function, for it is here that the Lord Mayor appears on the occasion of royal and other official processions.

The principal reception room is the Egyptian Hall. Visitors are also shown the Conference Room, with a fine stucco ceiling; the Saloon, with beautiful tapestries and a Waterford glass chandelier; the Drawing Rooms; and the tiny Court of Justice, with cells beneath.

To visit the Mansion House it is necessary to apply well in advance to the Private Secretary's Office, Mansion House, offering at least two alternative dates (which must be on Tues., Wed. or Thurs.).

Mansion House, residence of the Lord Mayor ▶

Marble Arch and Speakers' Corner   E3

Situation
Hyde Park

Underground station
Marble Arch

On an island site in the midst of London's rushing traffic stands Marble Arch, an imposing triumphal arch designed by John Nash on the model of the Arch of Constantine in Rome. Originally intended to serve as the main gateway to Buckingham Palace (see entry), it was found to be too narrow to admit the state coach and was moved in 1851 to its present site at the NE corner of Hyde Park (see entry). It stands close to Tyburn, which from the 12th c. to 1793 was London's place of execution; criminals were brought here from the Tower or from Newgate prison to end on the gallows ("Tyburn tree"). The site of Tyburn is marked by a small stone slab let into the roadway.

Speakers' Corner

Opposite Marble Arch is Speakers' Corner, a traditional forum of free speech where anyone with a grievance or a mission can find an audience. Speakers' Corner is particularly busy on Saturdays and Sunday afternoons, when numbers of soapbox orators address large groups of listeners or a few indifferent bystanders with equal eloquence. The speakers' themes are usually religious or political, and they are frequently exposed to lively heckling. Jomo Kenyatta, President of Kenya, spoke here in his younger days, and Idi Amin, later notorious as President of Uganda, was often a member of the crowd when he was an NCO in the British army.

Marble Arch

Speakers' Corner

Marlborough House and Queen's Chapel   F4

Marlborough House, now a Commonwealth conference and research centre, was built by Wren (1709–10) for Sarah, Duchess of Marlborough, and subsequently much altered and enlarged. It was occupied in the 19th c. by Prince Leopold, later Leopold I of the Belgians (1831), and in 1850 became the official residence of the Prince of Wales, occupied successively by the future Edward VII and George V. Queen Mary lived here from 1936 until her death in 1953. The house contains magnificent murals by the French painter Louis Laguerre, depicting the Duke of Marlborough's victories at Blenheim, Ramillies and Malplaquet.

In the grounds of Marlborough House is the Queen's Chapel, which belongs to St James's Palace (see entry), on the opposite side of Marlborough Street. The chapel was built by Inigo Jones for Charles I's queen, Henrietta Maria, and refurnished for Charles II's marriage to Catherine of Braganza in 1661. A hundred years later it was the scene of another royal wedding, when George III married Charlotte Sophia of Mecklenburg-Strelitz (1761).

Marlborough House and the Queen's Chapel can be seen only by prior arrangement with the Administration Officer (tel. 930 9249).

Address
Pall Mall, SW1

Underground station
Green Park

Opening times
Weekdays by prior arrangement with the Administration Officer

Admission charge

Middlesex Guildhall   G4

The former Middlesex Guildhall, a Renaissance-style building erected in 1913, now houses Middlesex Crown Court, with six court-rooms. Memorial panels in the entrance hall, with the

Address
Broad Sanctuary, SW1

Monument

signatures of King George of Greece, Queen Wilhelmina of the Netherlands and King Haakon of Norway, commemorate the fact that the court-rooms were used by the maritime courts of the Allies during the last war.

The site was once occupied by a tower marking the sanctuary of Westminster Abbey (see entry), within which the oppressed were safe from their pursuers. Thus Edward V was born in the sanctuary, in which his mother had sought refuge. The existence of the sanctuary is reflected in local street-names (Broad Sanctuary, Little Sanctuary).

---

*Monument   J3

Situation
Fish Street Hill, EC3

Underground station
Monument

Opening times
Apr.–Sept., Mon.–Sat. 9 a.m.–
5.40 p.m. (May–Sept. also
Sun. 2–5.40 p.m.); Oct.–Mar.,
Mon.–Sat. 9 a.m.–3.40 p.m.

Admission charge

This tall column, 61·5 m (202 ft) high, was erected between 1671 and 1677 to commemorate the Great Fire. It stands exactly 61·5 m (202 ft) from the spot in Pudding Lane where the fire started. Although attributed to Wren, it was probably designed by Robert Hooke. An internal spiral staircase of 311 steps leads up to a platform from which there is a magnificent view of London. The column is topped by an urn with a gilded flaming ball, 14 m (42 ft) high. The Monument is closed 1 Jan., Good Friday and 25–26 Dec., and sometimes closes at short notice.

---

*Museum of London   J2/3

Address
Barbican, London Wall, EC2

Underground stations
St Paul's, Barbican
(weekdays), Moorgate

Opening times
Tues.–Sat. 10 a.m.–6 p.m.,
Sun. 2–6 p.m.

Closed
1 Jan. 25–26 Dec. and Bank
Holidays

Admission free

The Museum of London, housed in a magnificently designed new building in the Barbican area of the City, was opened in 1976, bringing together the collections of the old London Museum, previously housed in Kensington Palace (see entry), and the Guildhall Museum.

The museum covers the whole range of London's history, with displays of Roman remains, including pottery and bronzes, Anglo-Saxon material, furniture, clothing, documents and musical instruments of the Tudor and Stuart periods, a cell from the old Newgate prison, reconstructions of Victorian and Edwardian shops and offices. There is an audio-visual presentation of the Great Fire of 1666, and exhibits illustrating the history of local authority services, schools and places of entertainment.

The most sumptuous exhibit, however, is the Lord Mayor's golden state coach, which leaves the museum once a year to drive through the streets of the City in the procession of the Lord Mayor's Show (see General, Election of Lord Mayor).

**National Gallery   G3

Address
Trafalgar Square, WC2

Underground station
Charing Cross

The National Gallery is one of the world's largest and finest collections of pictures. It is housed in a classical-style building by William Wilkins (1838), with an unimposing dome and pepper-box turrets which earned it the nickname of the "national cruet-stand". From the terrace there is a good view of Trafalgar Square and Whitehall (see entries). In front of the building is a statue (by Grinling Gibbons, 1686) of James II in

Museum of London: "Bull and Mouth" sign and shop fronts

National Gallery

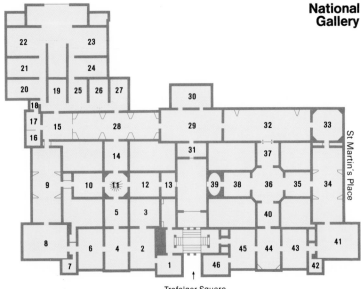

St Martin's Place

Trafalgar Square

1–2	Early Italian school	14	15th c. Italian school – Florence, Milan	31	Domenichino frescoes
3–6	15th c. Italian school – Florence	15	16th c. Italian school	32	17th c. French school
7	Leonardo da Vinci	16–19	17th c. Dutch school	33	18th c. French school
8	Correggio, Michelangelo, Parmigianino, Raphael	20–22	17th c. Flemish school	34	English school
		23	15th and early 16th c. German school	35	18th c. Italian school
9	16th c. Italian school – Venice	24	Dutch school	36	19th c. French school
10	15th c. Italian school – Venice	25	16th c. Dutch school and Holbein	37	17th c. Italian school
11	15th c. Italian altarpieces			38–39	18th c. Italian school
12	15th c. North Italian school and Central Italian school	26–28	17th c. Dutch school	40	19th c. French school
		29	17th c. Italian school	41	Spanish school
13	Crivelli	30	16th c. Italian school – Brescia	42	At present closed
				43–46	19th c. French school

Opening times
Mon.–Sat. 10 a.m.–6 p.m.,
Sun. 2–6 p.m.

Closed
1 Jan., Good Friday, 1st
Mon. in May, 24–26 Dec.

Admission free

the garb of a Roman emperor, with an inscription referring to him as king of England, Scotland, France and Ireland.

The National Gallery was founded in 1824, when Parliament voted £60,000 for the purchase of 38 pictures from the famous Angerstein collection. Numerous later purchases and donations made it necessary to enlarge the building in 1876, when the dome was built; and there were further extensions in 1887, 1927 and 1929. In recent years a new annexe has provided much-needed additional display space.

The National Gallery contains masterpieces of all schools and periods, but its greatest treasures are the works by Dutch masters and painters of the 15th and 16th c. Italian schools. Of the gallery's total holdings of more than 4500 pictures some

2000 are on display. Less famous works are hung in the Reserve Collections in the basement.

Space does not permit a full listing of the pictures to be seen in the various rooms; and this might in any event be misleading, since there are rearrangements from time to time. Here it is possible to give only a summary of the principal artists represented in the collection.

Italian: Duccio, Pisanello, Masaccio, Paolo Uccello, Piero della Francesca, Alesso Baldovinetti, Cosimo Tura, Andrea Mantegna, Antonello da Messina, Giovanni Bellini, Carlo Crivelli, Bramantino, Antonio del Pollaiuolo, Sandro Botticelli, Piero di Cosimo, Leonardo da Vinci, Michelangelo, Pietro Perugino, Raphael, Pontormo, Andrea del Sarto, Bronzino, Correggio, Giorgione, Titian, Tintoretto, Veronese, Giovanni Battista Moroni, Lorenzo Lotto, Sebastiano del Piombo, Caravaggio, Canaletto, Francesco Guardi, Giovanni Battista Tiepolo.

Flemish and Dutch: Jan van Eyck, Rogier van der Weyden, Robert Campin, Hans Memling, Dierk Bouts, Gerard David, Hieronymus Bosch, Pieter Bruegel, Rubens, van Dyck, Frans Hals, Rembrandt, Vermeer, Pieter de Hooch, Jacob van Ruisdael, Carel Fabritius, Gerard Terborch, Jan Steen, Hobbema.

German: Lucas Cranach, Dürer, Albrecht Altdorfer, Hans Holbein the Younger.

French: Master of St Gilles, Nicolas Poussin, Claude Lorrain, Louis le Nain, Philippe de Champaigne, Watteau, Chardin, Ingres, Delacroix, Daumier, Courbet, Manet, Degas, Cézanne, Renoir.

Spanish: El Greco, Velázquez, Zurbarán, Goya.

English: William Hogarth, Sir Joshua Reynolds, Gainsborough, Constable, Turner.

With so many pictures on display, no visitor can hope to do justice to them all. The best method is to consult the plan (above), decide which periods and schools you want to concentrate on and plan your visit accordingly.

*National Portrait Gallery   G3

The criterion for inclusion in the National Portrait Gallery is not so much the quality of the picture as a work of art as the fame of the person portrayed.

Founded in 1856 as a collection of portraits of notable personalities, the gallery now contains more than 4500 pictures, drawings and works of sculpture depicting people who have played a leading part in public life in Britain. No portraits are put on display until the person concerned has been dead for at least ten years; only members of the royal family are excepted from this rule.

For the most part the portraits are displayed in chronological order, beginning on the top floor (Rooms 1–15).

Address
St Martin's Place, Trafalgar Square, WC2

Underground stations
Charing Cross, Leicester Square

Opening times
Mon.–Fri. 10 a.m.–5 p.m., Sat. 10 a.m.–6 p.m., Sun. 2–6 p.m.

Closed
1 Jan., Good Friday, 1st Mon. in May, 24–26 Dec.

Admission free

National Postal Museum   H/J3

The National Postal Museum, opened in 1966 and extended in 1969, has a collection of some 350,000 stamps from all over

Address
King Edward Street, EC1

National Theatre

Underground station
St Paul's

Opening times
Mon.–Thurs. 10 a.m.–
4.30 p.m., Fri. 10 a.m.–4 p.m.

Admission free

the world, together with artists' drawings, philatelic books and documents on the history of the postal service.

The main elements in the museum are the Reginald M. Phillips collection of 19th c. British stamps, which covers the development, planning and issue of the world's first postage stamp – a British invention – and the Post Office's collection of British and foreign stamps.

---

*National Theatre   H3

Address
South Bank, SE1

Underground stations
Waterloo, Embankment

In 1976 the National Theatre Company, founded in 1963, acquired a home of its own in the new South Bank development; until then it had been temporarily accommodated in the historic Old Vic theatre in Waterloo Road. The National Theatre, lying close to the S end of Waterloo Bridge, forms part of the South Bank arts centre which also includes the Royal Festival Hall (see entry), Queen Elizabeth Hall and Purcell Room, the National Film Theatre with its two cinemas and the Hayward Gallery (see entry) of modern art. Designed by Sir Denys Lasdun, it is a massive concrete structure containing three theatres with a total of 2400 seats, a restaurant seating more than 1000, eight bars, 135 air-conditioned dressing rooms, scenery and wardrobe stores, offices, workshops and parking for 400 cars, together with foyers, galleries and ample circulation space. In the interior decoration full use is made of concrete as a stylistic element. Although the first effect may be confusing, the theatre is excellently planned

National Theatre

so as to allow both actors and theatre-goers to get from place to place as quickly as possible.

The Lyttleton Theatre (named after the Lyttleton family who promoted the idea of a National Theatre) has 895 seats, a large stage, sophisticated machinery and equipment and good sight-lines. In some parts of the house, however, the acoustics leave something to be desired.

The Olivier Theatre, the largest of the three, has 1160 seats and an open, revolving stage; but here, too, there have been complaints about the acoustics in certain parts of the house.

The Cottesloe Theatre (named after Lord Cottesloe, first chairman of the National Theatre) is an experimental theatre or theatre workshop, with a central stage or acting area around which 200 to 400 seats can be arranged according to requirements.

The establishment of the National Theatre was designed to provide a suitable forum for British dramatists from Shakespeare to contemporary playwrights, but this was only one part of its task. It was also expected to send out touring productions to the provinces and to other countries and to invite foreign companies to perform in London. The two larger theatres house not only productions by the National Theatre Company but also performances by such foreign companies as the Schaubühne of Berlin and the Théâtre National Populaire of Paris, while in the small Cottesloe Theatre can be seen experimental and avant-garde productions by touring companies from all over the country.

Laurence Olivier (Lord Olivier), first director of the National Theatre, developed a comprehensive programme of all kinds of dramatic productions with a first-rate company; and his successor, Peter Hall, has continued the tradition, at the same time extending the scope of the National Theatre's activities to obviate the risk of cultural isolation. Thus even when the theatres themselves are not functioning there are likely to be performances going on in other parts of the building: this was the architect's intention, as it is the director's. These additional events – pop and folk music, jazz, medieval music, street theatre, etc. – have proved extremely popular. Every evening before curtain-up in the theatre there is a musical programme in the foyer, ranging from classical music to jazz, and theatregoers now come early in order to be present at these performances.

On certain days of the week there are also "platform shows" in the Lyttleton Theatre, when, on a temporary stage in front of the curtain, members of the National Theatre Company or guest artistes put on a programme which may range from poetry readings to mime, from a puppet show to a song recital.

*Natural History Museum C4

The original nucleus of the Natural History Museum, which was founded in 1754 and moved into its present building in 1881, was formed by the scientific collections of Sir Hans Sloane. The Museum is a palatial building in Romanesque style (1873–80), 230 m (675 ft) long, with two 64 m (190 ft) high towers. The exterior is faced with terracotta slabs bearing relief figures of animals. Proposals for the partial reconstruction of the building have recently given rise to controversy.

Address
Cromwell Road, South Kensington, SW7

Underground stations
Gloucester Road, South Kensington

Opening times
Mon.–Sat. 10 a.m.–6 p.m.,
Sun. 2.30–6 p.m.

Closed
1 Jan., Good Friday, 1st
Mon. in May, 24–26 Dec.

Admission free

The Natural History Museum, which is officially part of the British Museum (see entry), has five departments, each with its own library and reading rooms – Zoology, Mineralogy, Botany, Entomology and Palaeontology.

The department of palaeontology is housed in the E wing of the ground floor, with a collection of fossils illustrating the development of the animal kingdom – the selection and adaptation of particular species, the links between fossils and living species, the principles of classification of organic life (demonstrated by the lower animals and fishes) and finally the development of man.

Beyond the broad staircase is the North Hall, which is mainly used for special exhibitions.

In the Central Hall the museum's famous models and fossil remains of dinosaurs, reptiles and birds have been recently rearranged.

In the W wing is the Bird Gallery, with a special room devoted to British birds. This is the beginning of the department of zoology, which is continued in the rooms to the N of the Bird Gallery – the Reptile Gallery, the Fish Gallery and the very interesting Starfish Gallery.

Here, too, is the Insect Gallery, and beyond this the Whale Hall, with skeletons and models of these largest of living mammals. The star exhibit in this gallery is a life-size cast of a blue whale, 27 m (91 ft) long.

On the first floor a Mammal Gallery houses such rarities as the okapi, platypus and Tasmanian devil.

The Mineral Gallery has a collection of some 130,000 specimens, representing about 75% of the world's known minerals. Also in this gallery is a collection of some 1270 specimens of meteorites, including the huge Cranbourne meteorite from Australia which weighs $3\frac{1}{2}$ tons.

On the second floor is the Botanical Gallery.

---

*Old Bailey (Central Criminal Court) H3

Address
Newgate Street/Old Bailey,
EC4

Underground station
St Paul's

The massive building officially known as the Central Criminal Court (built 1902–7), the principal criminal court for Greater London, is more commonly referred to as the Old Bailey, after the name of the street in which it stands. On top of the dome is a figure of Justice, with her sword and scales, but not blindfolded. The building was restored after suffering severe damage during the last war.

Until 1903 the site of the Old Bailey was occupied by Newgate Prison, for a long time London's chief prison. From 1783 to 1868 public executions were carried out in front of the prison. For admission to sittings of the courts (at 10.15 a.m. and 1.45 p.m. daily) apply at the Newgate Street entrance or at the entrance to the public gallery in Old Bailey.

**Piccadilly Circus F3

Underground station
Piccadilly Circus

Piccadilly Circus is one of the great centres of London life and one of its noisiest and busiest traffic intersections, situated at the meeting of five major streets. The many night spots in the

Natural History Museum: the Whale Hall

Old Bailey

surrounding area make it the heart of the West End world of entertainment. It is thus equally busy by night and by day.

In the centre of the Circus stands the Shaftesbury Memorial, commemorating the philanthropic 7th Earl of Shaftesbury (by Sir Alfred Gilbert, 1893). This is a bronze fountain topped by a cast aluminium figure of an archer, universally known as Eros although in fact the figure was intended to represent the angel of Christian charity.

Piccadilly, one of London's most fashionable streets, runs W from the Circus. It is named after the "picadils" (ruffs) made by a well-known 18th c. tailor.

Post Office Tower   F2

Address
Maple Street, W1
Underground stations
Goodge St, Warren Street,
Great Portland Street

The Post Office Tower, built in 1966, rises to a height of 177 m (580 ft) above the surrounding streets. It houses both a television transmitter and receiver and a radio-telephone relay. Two lifts ascend to the top which is crowned by an aerial mast. The tower is not open to the public.

*Regent's Park   D/E1/2

Underground stations
Baker Street, Regent's Park,
Great Portland Street

Originally a royal hunting ground, Regent's Park was laid out in its present form by John Nash and is now a popular place of recreation, with an artificial lake, also designed by Nash (boats for hire), a small boating pond for children, tennis courts, a cricket ground and children's playgrounds. There are also an

In Regent's Park, one of London's open spaces   *Piccadilly Circus* ▶

open-air theatre, in which performances of Shakespeare plays and pop concerts are given in summer, and the beautiful Queen Mary's Gardens (rose-garden, rockery) with a restaurant and cafeteria.

The greatest attraction in Regent's Park, however, is the Zoo (see entry), which lies on the N side of the park and is reached by way of the Broad Walk.

The Outer Circle, a carriage-drive encircling the park, has on its E, S and W sides the famous "Nash terraces" – uniform streets of houses in monumental classical style. Particularly impressive is Park Crescent, at the SE corner of the park on the far side of Marylebone Road. Much other work by Nash can be seen in central London, particularly in the area between Regent's Park and Buckingham Palace.

*Richmond Park

Underground stations
Richmond, Putney Bridge

British Rail station
Richmond

Thames launches
Richmond

Opening times
7 a.m. to dusk

With an area of some 660 ha (2300 acres), Richmond Park is the largest city park in Britain and the one with the oldest oaks. The old town of Richmond, in the area of which it lies, situated on the south-western outskirts of London on the S bank of the Thames, is one of the 32 London boroughs and one of the city's most favoured residential suburbs.

The park was enclosed by Charles I in 1637 as a deer-park, and numbers of red and fallow deer still roam at large in its well-wooded expanses, while the Pen Ponds, excavated in the 18th c., are the haunt of waterfowl of all kinds. On the E side of the park, facing Roehampton, are two public golf-courses, and on the W side are attractive footpaths over Ham and Petersham commons. Among the most attractive features of the park are the Isabella Plantations, a woodland garden laid out in 1831, and the Prince Charles Spinney, in which some 5300 trees (oak, beech, chestnut, ash and maple) were planted in 1949.

The park has ten gates, and contains a number of old mansions. Near the Roehampton Gate is White Lodge, built by George II as a hunting lodge, in which the Duke of Windsor (Edward VIII) was born and the Duke of York lived before his accession as George VI. The house is now occupied by the Royal Ballet School. It is open to visitors on weekdays in August.

Royal Academy   F3

Address
Piccadilly, W1

Underground stations
Piccadilly Circus, Green Park

Opening times
Daily 10 a.m.–6 p.m.

The Royal Academy of Arts, founded in 1768 under the patronage of George II, has been housed since 1869 in Burlington House, an imposing mansion with a Renaissance-style façade. The Academy's first president was Sir Joshua Reynolds, whose statue stands in the courtyard.

The Royal Academy is a self-governing and self-supporting society of artists with a membership of 50 Royal Academicians and 25 Associates, all painters, sculptors, graphic artists and architects. At the age of 70 a Royal academician becomes a Senior Academician, and his successor is elected from among the Associates. Election to the Royal Academy was for long the peak of an artist's career, holding the prospect of wealth and not infrequently a title.

Royal Academy

Bank of England, Stock Exchange and Royal Exchange

The Academy's art school in Burlington House has had such distinguished pupils as Constable, Lawrence, Turner and Millais. Every year between May and August it mounts a summer exhibition of work by contemporary British artists. Only work done within the past ten years is eligible, and the competition is fierce, no more than 1500 of the 11,000 or so works submitted being accepted by the jury. The Royal Academy attracts international attention, however, with its great special exhibitions devoted to a particular theme – China, Pompeii, Turner, "The Gold of Eldorado", etc.

Various special exhibitions are also put on in the private apartments of the Academy, which are not normally open to the public, and these provide an opportunity of seeing the Academy's greatest treasure, the Michelangelo Tondo. This relief of the Virgin and Child with the infant John the Baptist, the only piece of sculpture by Michelangelo in Britain, is carved from white Carrara marble and measures 1·1 m (3½ ft) across. It was created by Michelangelo, immediately after his "David", for the patrician Taddeo Taddei and remained in the Taddei family until the early 19th c. It was then purchased by a well-known British collector, Sir George Beaumont, and presented to the Royal Academy after his death.

*Royal Festival Hall G3

Address
South Bank, SE1

Underground stations
Embankment, Waterloo

The Royal Festival Hall, one of London's finest concert halls, is part of a modern centre of the arts created on the South Bank of the Thames, close to Waterloo Bridge, between 1951 and 1976 – fulfilling a long cherished wish of the London County Council to redevelop and revitalise this once rather run-down area of the city.

In addition to the Royal Festival Hall the complex includes two smaller concert halls (the Queen Elizabeth Hall and the Purcell Room), the Hayward Gallery (see entry) of modern art, the National Film Theatre, with two cinemas, and the National Theatre (see entry) with its three auditoriums. Some visitors may find the bare concrete structures of these buildings rather

Royal Festival Hall and Shell Building

Royal Festival Hall at night

cold and bleak, but from the functional standpoint they are excellently adapted to their purpose.

The Royal Festival Hall, designed by Sir Robert Matthew and J. M. Martin and built between 1951 and 1965, can seat an audience of 3400 and has two terrace restaurants. Its acoustics are first-class, providing ideal conditions for both orchestral and choral performances.

The Queen Elizabeth Hall, with a smaller concert hall (seating 1100) for symphony concerts and the Purcell Room (seating 270) for chamber music and solo recitals, was opened in 1967.

---

*Royal Mews   E/F4

In the Royal Mews visitors can see an array of state coaches and carriages used by British monarchs, some of them still in use on state occasions. Here, too, the horses which draw them are stabled (though the horses are not always there). The finest items in the collection are the golden state coach designed for George III and still used at coronations; the Irish state coach, purchased by Queen Victoria in 1852, in which the monarch drives to the state opening of Parliament; and the glass coach, acquired by George V in 1910, which is used principally for royal weddings.

The harness of the golden state coach is claimed to be the finest in the world.

A number of Rolls-Royce Phantom Vs are also on display.

Address
Buckingham Palace Road, SW1

Underground station
Victoria

Opening times
Wed. and Thurs. 2–4 p.m.

Closed
During Ascot week (June)

Admission charge

The Golden State Carriage

St Bartholomew the Great Church   H/J2

Address
West Smithfield, EC1

Underground stations
Barbican, St Paul's

Opening times
9 a.m. to dusk

St Bartholomew the Great, the City's oldest parish church, is an impressive example of Norman church architecture, with round arches and billet moulding running continuously from pier to pier in the choir.

The church, originally belonging to an Augustinian priory, was founded by a monk named Rahere in 1123. The transepts were added at the end of the 12th c., and the church was rebuilt in Early English style about 1300. At the Reformation the nave was pulled down and the original choir became the parish church. During the 18th c. the church was used as a warehouse, a store, an inn and a blacksmith's forge. Thereafter it was restored, incorporating parts of the older church, and brought back into use for worship.

The most notable feature within the church is the tomb of the founder and first prior, with a recumbent figure of Rahere clad in the black robe of an Augustinian canon and flanked by small kneeling figures of monks holding books inscribed with texts from Isaiah; at his feet is a crowned angel holding a shield with the arms of the priory. The figure of Rahere is 12th c.; the canopy over the tomb and the wall facing are 15th c.

Also of interest are the Lady Chapel (built 1410, restored at end of 19th c.); the altar tomb of Sir Walter Mildmay, chancellor of the exchequer under Elizabeth I; the early 15th c. font; and the

St Bartholomew the Great ▶

cloister (built 1405, restored in the original style 1905–28),
which is entered by a Norman doorway with 15th c. doors.
The churchyard occupies the site of the destroyed nave. The
13th c. gateway was originally the entrance to the S aisle.
Services are held every Sunday at 9 a.m., 11 a.m. and 6.30 p.m.

St Bride's Church   H3

Address
Fleet Street, EC4

Underground station
Blackfriars

Opening times
9 a.m.–5 p.m.

St Bride's, dedicated to the 6th c. Irish saint Bride or Bridget, is
the parish church of the Press. The church is first mentioned in
the records in the 12th c.
St Bride's has a fine 16th c. font and a carved oak reredos. The
crypt houses an interesting little museum, with a Roman
pavement, remains of earlier churches and an exhibition
illustrating the history of the church, with particular emphasis
on its associations with the Press.

St Clement Danes Church   H3

Address
Strand, WC2

Underground station
Temple

Designed by Wren and built in 1681, the church was gutted by
bombing during the last war, only the tower (by James Gibb,
1719) remaining unscathed. It was restored in the original style
in 1958.
The church *may* derive its name from the fact that there was a
Danish settlement on the site before the Norman Conquest.
St Clement Danes is the official church of the Royal Air Force. It
contains the roll of honour, bearing the names of more than
125,000 members of the RAF who lost their lives in the Second
World War, and reproductions of the crests of more than 700
RAF units.
The bells of St Clement Danes, long familiar to children in an
old nursery rhyme ("Oranges and lemons, say the bells of St
Clement's"), ring daily at 9 a.m., noon, 3 p.m. and 6 p.m. Every
year in March there is a special children's service, when each
child is given an orange and a lemon on leaving the church.

*St Helen's Church   K3

Address
Great St Helen's,
Bishopsgate, EC3

Underground station
Liverpool Street

St Helen's is one of the finest and most interesting churches in
the City. Originally built in the 12th c., it was altered between
the 13th and 14th c., and has been preserved mainly in its 14th
c. form. It has two parallel naves of equal size, one originally
reserved for the nuns of the convent to which the church
belonged, the other for the lay congregation.
Features of particular interest are the monument of Sir
John Spencer, Lord Mayor of London (1608), on the S wall;
the pulpit and altar; the canopied tomb of Sir William Pickering,
ambassador to France in the 16th c.; and the table-tomb of Sir
John Crosby (d. 1475).

*St James's Palace

Not far away from Buckingham Palace (see entry) is the older St James's Palace, part of a group of buildings which includes Clarence House and Lancaster House. The palace contains a number of "grace and favour" apartments occupied by royal pensioners. To the SE, beyond the magnificent avenue of the Mall, is St James's Park (see entry); to the SW of the palace is Green Park.

In spite of later destruction and alteration, the palace still offers a fine example of brick-built Tudor architecture. It takes its name from a leper hospital dedicated to St James the Less which stood here from the 12th c. until 1532.

The old hospital was pulled down by Henry VIII and replaced by a palace designed by Holbein, in which Charles II, James II, Mary II, Anne and George IV were born. After the burning down of the old palace of Whitehall in 1699 (see Banqueting House) St James's Palace became the official residence of the monarch until it gave place to Buckingham Palace (see entry); foreign ambassadors are still accredited to the "court of St James's".

The main relic of the Tudor palace is the Gatehouse or Clock Tower, in St James's Street, which leads into the Colour Court, with a 17th c. colonnade.

The palace has two chapels. In the Ambassadors' Court (to the W of the Gatehouse) is the entrance to the Chapel Royal, built in 1532 but with much later alteration. The fine paintings on the coffered ceiling are attributed to Holbein. Other notable features are the royal pew, the 17th c. panelling and the richly ornamented roof. In this chapel were celebrated the marriages of William and Mary (1677), Queen Anne (1683), George IV (1795), Victoria (1840) and George V (1893).

The other chapel, the Queen's Chapel, is in Marlborough Street (see Marlborough House).

On the N side of the Ambassadors' Court stands York House, which was occupied in 1915–16 by Lord Kitchener and from 1919 to 1930 by the Prince of Wales, later Duke of Windsor; it is now the residence of the Duke of Gloucester.

St James's Palace is also the headquarters of the Queen's bodyguard, consisting of the Yeomen of the Guard and the Honourable Corps of Gentlemen at Arms. The Yeomen of the Guard, a corps established by Henry VII in 1485, are popularly known as Beefeaters (probably a corruption of the French "Buffetiers du Roi"). The Corps of Gentlemen at Arms, founded in 1509 by Henry VIII, is made up of distinguished army officers under a captain appointed by the government of the day.

Address
Pall Mall, SW1

Underground station
Green Park

Opening times
Not open to public

Clarence House

On the W side of the group of buildings around St James's Palace is Clarence House, a stucco-fronted mansion built by John Nash for the Duke of Clarence, later William IV. Before her accession it was the official London residence of Princess Elizabeth and the Duke of Edinburgh; and is now the home of Queen Elizabeth the Queen Mother.

Lancaster House

Lancaster House

On the opposite side of Stable Yard from Clarence House is Lancaster House, now used for government receptions, banquets and conferences. It was begun by Benjamin Wyatt in 1825 for the Duke of York, who died before the house was completed, leaving enormous debts. In 1840 it was finished by Sir Robert Smirke and Sir Charles Barry and acquired by one of the Duke's creditors, the Marquess of Stafford (later Duke of Sutherland), who renamed it Stafford House. In the early years of the 20th c. it was presented to the nation by the first Lord Leverhulme as a home for the London Museum and given its present name. It was occupied by the museum from 1914 to 1951.

The magnificence of the state apartments led Queen Victoria to say to the Duchess of Sutherland, "I have come from my house to your palace."

The two-storeyed portico leads into the vestibule, to the left of which is the Garibaldi Room (commemorating Garibaldi's stay in the house in 1864), with a fine marble fireplace and Italian mirror. To the left of this is the East Dining Room, to the right the State Dining Room, richly decorated, with a clock which belonged to Napoleon I. On the other side of this room are the Red Room, Gold Room and Library.

Address
Stable Yard, St James's Palace, SW1

Underground station
Green Park

Opening times
Easter Sat. to mid-Dec., Sat., Sun. and public holidays 2–6 p.m.

Admission charge

◀ *St James's Palace*

Adjoining is the splendid Staircase Hall, rising to the full height of the building, with a Rococo-style balustrade.

On the first floor are the recently renovated state apartments. The West Drawing Room, formerly the Duchess's boudoir, has a ceiling painting of the solar system; the State Drawing Room has a fine coffered ceiling and fireplaces. The Great Gallery, 40 m (120 ft) long, notable for its elaborate decoration, has a painting by Guercino. The Veronese Room has a ceiling painting by Paul Veronese.

St James's Park   F4

Situation
The Mall, SW1

Underground stations
St James's Park, Charing Cross, Green Park

St James's Park, London's most attractive park, is a masterpiece of landscape architecture by John Nash, aimed at achieving the unspoiled natural effect of an English park, like those to be found in the counties of Kent, Hampshire or Sussex. Originally a marshy area of meadowland, it was drained in the reign of Henry VIII and made into a deer-park. The French landscape gardener Le Nôtre laid it out as a pleasure ground for Charles II. In 1829 Nash gave the park its present aspect, forming a lake with islands which provide nesting places for many species of waterfowl. The birds to be seen here include pelicans.

From the bridge over the lake there are fine views of Buckingham Palace (see entry) to the W and the buildings lining Whitehall (see entry) to the E.

St James's Park

St John's Gate and St John's Church   H2

St John's Gate was originally the main entrace to a priory of the
order of St John of Jerusalem (the Knights Hospitallers).
Dating from 1504, it is the only surviving remnant of the priory.
The rooms above the gateway are now the headquarters of the
revived Order of the Hospital of St John of Jerusalem, and
contain a small museum.

The order, founded in Jerusalem in the 11th c., and later based
successively in Cyprus, Rhodes and Malta, came to England in
the 12th c. and built a priory in London in 1148. After being
burned down in 1381 this was re-erected in 1504. The order
was suppressed in England in 1537, but was re-founded about
1840 as a Protestant Grand Priory and recognised by Queen
Victoria about 1888.

The site of the priory church of 1185 is now occupied by St
John's Church (1721–3) in St John's Square, which
incorporates the choir walls of the old 12th and 16th c. church.
The church was damaged in the Second World War but was
completely restored in 1958. Its most notable features are the
15th c. altarpiece, depicting the victory of the Knights of St
John over the Turks during the Turkish siege of Rhodes, and
the Norman Crypt (1140–80), which has survived the hazards
of the centuries.

Address
St John's Lane, Clerkenwell,
EC1

Underground station
Farringdon

Opening times
Tues., Fri. and Sat. 10 a.m.–6
p.m.

Conducted tours
11 a.m. and 2.30 p.m.

Admission free

St Katharine's Dock   K3

This old dockland area, excellently restored and with an
interesting collection of historic ships, is increasingly
becoming one of London's tourist attractions.

St Katharine's Dock was inaugurated in 1827 with a parade of
gaily decorated sailing ships, but, as time went on and ships
grew larger than it could handle, its fortunes declined. Finally in
the 1960s the Greater London Council's plans for the
rehabilitation of London's dockland without fundamentally
altering its character gave the area a new lease of life. Some of
the handsome old warehouses were converted into flats, and
other buildings were restored, including the Dockmaster's
House, the Dickens Inn (1800: now a pub and restaurant) and
the Italian-style Ivory House. New buildings have been erected
behind old façades, such as International House (still under
construction), which has replaced an old warehouse destroyed
by fire, preserving the original front wall. Here, too, have been
established institutions such as the World Trade Centre, and
this has led to the construction of additional hotels. In this way
the whole area, which was threatening to degenerate into a
slum, has taken on fresh life in its new form.

The docks themselves now provide moorings for more than
200 private yachts and other vessels and are the headquarters
of a yacht club (of which visitors can become temporary
members). Here, too, is the Maritime Trust's Historic Ship
Collection, including the Nore lightship (1931); the "Chal-
lenge", at the time of its launch (1931) the most modern tug of
its day; the "Lizzie Porter", a motor-driven lifeboat built in 1909
and the "Cambria", a thames barge built in 1906 which was the

Address
St Katharine's Way, E1

Underground stations
Tower Hill, Aldgate, Aldgate
East

St Katharine Docks

last British vessel trading under sail alone. The centrepiece of the collection, however, is Captain Scott's polar research ship the "Discovery", which took him on his first voyage to the Antarctic in 1901. In the course of his second voyage (1910), on which he reached the South Pole only three weeks after the Norwegian explorer Amundsen (18 January 1912), Scott and his companions perished. Visitors are shown Scott's cabin on the "Discovery".

St Margaret's Church, Westminster   G4

Address
Parliament Square, SW1

Underground stations
Westminster, St James's Park

Opening times
Weekdays 9 a.m.–4 p.m.

St Margaret's, the parish church of the House of Commons and the scene of many fashionable weddings, was founded in the 11th or 12th c., rebuilt in 1523 by Robert Stowell, master-mason of Westminster Abbey (see entry), refaced in 1735 and restored by Sir George Gilbert Scott in 1878.

The church is notable particularly for the Flemish stained glass in the E window, presented by Ferdinand and Isabella of Spain on the occasion of the marriage of Prince Arthur, Henry VIII's elder brother, to Catherine of Aragon. Before the glass arrived in London Arthur had died and Henry had married his widow: whereupon the glass was sent to Waltham Abbey, coming to St Margaret's only in 1758.

Other features of interest are the altarpiece, the centre panel of which is a carving of the Supper at Emmaus, copied from Titian's picture; 16th and 17th c. memorial brasses (including one to Sir Walter Raleigh, the founder of Virginia); and Elizabethan and Jacobean monuments.

St Martin-in-the-Fields Church · G3

St Martin-in-the-Fields is the royal parish church (hence the royal coat of arms above the Corinthian portico), and also the parish church of the Admiralty, and accordingly flies the naval flag, the white ensign, on state occasions.

There has been a church on this site since 1222 at least. The original church was rebuilt in the reign of Henry VIII (1544) and replaced in 1726 by the present structure, designed by James Gibbs, a pupil of Wren's. The church is Gibbs's masterpiece, notable particularly for its Corinthian portico, its 56 m (185 ft) high steeple and its elliptical ceiling (of Italian workmanship), supported on Corinthian columns. The font belonged to the previous church, of which there are some other relics in the crypt (worth seeing for its own sake, with massive square piers). To the N of the altar is the royal box or pew, to the S the Admiralty box. Above the chancel arch are the arms of George I.

A notable vicar (from 1914 to 1927) of the church was Dick Sheppard – notable both for his preaching and for his social welfare work. For many years the church's crypt offered shelter for the night to the destitute and homeless.

Address
Trafalgar Square, WC2
Underground stations
Charing Cross, Leicester Square, Embankment
Opening times
Daily 7.30 a.m.–8 p.m.

St Martin-in-the-Fields

St Mary-le-Bow Church · J3

The City church of St Mary-le-Bow, with its famous bells, occupies a special place in the affections of Londoners. To be a genuine Cockney, it is said, you must have been born within the sound of Bow bells.

The church, originally a Norman foundation and one of London's oldest stone churches, was rebuilt by Wren between 1670 and 1683. It suffered heavy damage during the Second World War and was re-dedicated after extensive restoration in 1964. Its most notable feature is the 73 m (221 ft) high steeple containing the bells which is topped by a weathervane nearly 3 m (9 ft) high.

Address
Cheapside, EC2

Underground stations
St Paul's, Bank, Mansion House

Opening times
Mon.–Sat. 8.45 a.m.–4 p.m.

St Mary-le-Strand Church · G3

The church of St Mary-le-Strand stands in the middle of the Strand opposite Somerset House (see entry), within easy reach of the Victoria Embankment, which runs along the N bank of the Thames between Westminster Bridge and Blackfriars Bridge. Just along the Strand to the E is the church of St Clement Danes (see entry), and beyond this is Fleet Street, with the Temple (see entries) immediately adjoining.

St Mary-le-Strand, a masterpiece of Baroque church architecture, was built by James Gibbs in 1714–17. Finely and rigorously proportioned, it is notable for its graceful steeple and unusual coffered ceiling.

Address
Strand, WC2

Underground station
Temple

St Paul's Cathedral H/J3

Address
St Paul's Churchyard, EC4

Underground stations
St Paul's, Mansion House

Opening times
Oct. to Easter, 8 a.m.–5 p.m.;
Easter to Sept., 8 a.m.–6 p.m.

Conducted tours
Mon.–Sat. 11 a.m. and
2 p.m.

Admission free

St Paul's Cathedral, seat of the Bishop of London and "parish church of the British Commonwealth", is the largest and most famous of the City's churches.

There has been a church on this site since very early times. The best known of the predecessors of the present cathedral, and in its day one of the richest churches in the world, was Old St Paul's, a great Gothic church with a spire 170 m (500 ft) high which was bady damaged by fire in 1561, partly rebuilt by Inigo Jones in 1627–42 and finally destroyed in the Great Fire (1666).

The present cathedral, begun in 1675 and completed in 1711, was designed by Wren. The plan was approved only after long wrangling with the church commissioners, who turned down Wren's first two designs. The result was a compromise between Wren's original idea of a dome and the commissioners' preference for a plan in the form of a Latin cross.

As finally built, however, St Paul's is Wren's masterpiece – a harmoniously proportioned Renaissance church 170 m (515 ft) long and 75 m (227 ft) wide across the transepts, with two Baroque towers 67 m (212 ft) high and a magnificent dome rising to a total height of 111 m (365 ft).

Since the repair of damage suffered by the cathedral during the last war and the cleaning of the façade to remove the accumulated grime of 250 years, St Paul's has been restored to its original majestic beauty, and even the external sculptured decoration by Francis Bird, Edward Pierce and Grinling Gibbons can be seen and appreciated.

St Paul's Cathedral

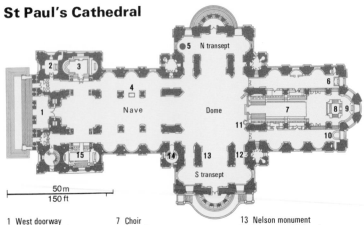

1 West doorway	7 Choir	13 Nelson monument
2 All Souls Chapel	8 High altar	14 Steps up to Whispering
3 St Dunstan's Chapel	9 American Memorial Chapel	Gallery, Library and Dome
4 Wellington monument	10 Lady Chapel	15 Chapel of St Michael and St
5 Font	11 Pulpit	George
6 Chapel of Modern Martyrs	12 Steps down to Crypt	

St Paul's Cathedral: interior ▶

St Paul's Cathedral

(1) The W front, with the main entrance, is 60 m (180 ft) long and has a columned portico surmounted by an upper colonnade. The relief on the pediment of the Conversion of St Paul, the statue of St Paul above the pediment and the two flanking statues of SS. James and Peter are by Francis Bird.

On either side of the portico are two similar Baroque towers. In the left-hand one is a peal of 12 bells, in the right-hand one the largest bell in England, Great Paul, weighing almost 17 tons (cast in 1882).

A flight of marble steps leads up into the cathedral. At the far end of the nave, which is slightly higher than the lateral aisles, the visitor's eye is caught at once by the great dome, borne on eight massive double piers with Corinthian capitals which are buttressed by four subsidiary piers.

(2) To the left is All Souls' Chapel, which since 1925 has been a memorial chapel to Field Marshal Lord Kitchener (d. 1916).

(3) Adjoining is St Dunstan's Chapel, which is reserved for private prayer. It has a 17th c. oak screen and a mosaic by Salviati.

(4) In the N aisle is an imposing monument to the Duke of Wellington (d. 1852) by Alfred Stevens.

(5) The N transept, with a fine font and statues of Sir Joshua Reynolds and Dr Samuel Johnson, was damaged by a bomb in 1941 and rebuilt in 1962.

(6) At the end of the N choir aisle is the Chapel of Modern Martyrs.

(7) We now enter the choir, with choir-stalls by Grinling Gibbons; particularly fine are the oblong panels with carved foliage ornament in pear-wood.

(8) The magnificent high altar with its baldacchino (canopy) is modern, designed by Dykes Bower and Godfrey Allen on the basis of sketches by Wren.

(9) Behind the high altar is the American Memorial Chapel or Jesus Chapel, destroyed in the Second World War and rebuilt in 1958. In the chapel is a roll of honour with the names of 28,000 Americans who fell during operations based on Britain.

(10) In the S choir aisle are the Lady Chapel and a statue of the poet John Donne, the only monument in Old St Paul's which survived the Great Fire.

(11) The pulpit, at the SW corner of the choir, is a splendid piece of woodcarving. In the massive double pier supporting the dome is the dean's vestry.

(12) From the vestry a flight of steps leads down into the crypt, which occupies the whole area under the cathedral and contains the tombs of many notable figures.

(13) The Nelson monument has allegorical reliefs representing the North Sea, the Baltic, the Mediterranean and the Nile.

(14) In the SW double pier is the staircase leading up to the Whispering Gallery, the Library and the Dome. Before climbing to the upper parts of the cathedral, however, the tour of the nave should be completed by a visit to the Chapel of St Michael and St George.

(15) This is the chapel of the Order of St Michael and St George (instituted in 1818), an honour conferred for service in Commonwealth and foreign affairs.

No visit to St Paul's would be complete without the climb to the galleries and dome.

A flight of 143 steps leads up to the South Triforium Gallery, which contains plans, models, etc. of earlier churches.

St Paul's Cathedral

The West Gallery leads into the Trophy Room, with Wren's first rejected plans for St Paul's and other drawings and relics.

Another 116 steps lead up to the Whispering Gallery, which runs round the dome at a height of 33 m (100 ft) above the ground. It is so called because of its remarkable acoustic properties, which make it possible to hear even a whisper across the dome's total width of 35 m (112 ft). From here visitors can see the paintings in the dome and gain a breathtaking impression of the size and proportions of the nave below.

From the Whispering Gallery a further 117 steps lead up to the Stone Gallery round the outside of the dome; and 166 steps above this is the Golden Gallery. From both of these galleries there are superb views of London.

*St Paul's Church, Covent Garden
G3

"The handsomest barn in England" Inigo Jones called this church, which he built in 1633. It is popularly known as the church "with the front at the back", since the portico facing Covent Garden Market square, which looks like the main front, is in fact the E end, while the main entrance is at the W end. St Paul's is also known as the "actors' church"; and until the removal of the old fruit, vegetable and flower market to a new site an annual harvest thanksgiving service was held in the church.

Address
Covent Garden, WC2

Underground station
Covent Garden

The church contains the graves of many noted Londoners of the 18th and 19th c., including many actors and actresses. In this respect it is surpassed only by Westminster Abbey and St Paul's Cathedral (see entries). It contains many interesting monuments and memorial tablets, as well as a carved wreath by Grinling Gibbons above the W door (1721).

Savoy Chapel   G3

Address
Savoy Hill, Strand, WC2

Underground stations
Embankment, Temple,
Charing Cross

Opening times
Tues.–Fri. 11 a.m.–3.30 p.m.

Closed
1 Jan., Easter Monday,
Aug.–Sept., 24 Dec.

The Savoy Chapel – officially the Queen's Chapel of the Savoy – stands in a side street off the Strand, near Waterloo Bridge. It is the private chapel of the sovereign since, as Duke of Lancaster, the monarch is the successor to John of Gaunt, Duke of Lancaster (1340–99).

John of Gaunt's palace, which once stood here, was razed to the ground during the Peasants' Revolt of 1381, though part of it was later rebuilt by Henry VII.

The late Perpendicular chapel was built in 1505, and after its destruction by fire in 1864 was rebuilt in the original style. It is the chapel of the Royal Victorian Order, membership of which is in the personal gift of the sovereign. At the W end of the chapel are the very fine royal pews.

*Science Museum   D4

Address
Exhibition Road, South
Kensington, SW7 2DD

Underground station
South Kensington

Opening times
Mon.–Sat. 10 a.m.–6 p.m.,
Sun. 2.30–6 p.m.

Closed
1 Jan., Good Friday, 1st
Mon. in May, 24–26 Dec.

Admission free

The extensive collections of the Science Museum form an impressive illustration of the function of science in understanding and explaining the phenomena, the processes and the laws of nature and in providing the theoretical basis for the practical application of the results achieved. Models and displays, experimental apparatus and original pieces of equipment show the process of putting theoretical advances into practice and illustrate the progress of science and technology over the centuries.

The various departments and galleries, on five floors (lower ground floor, ground floor, first, second and third floors), are excellently arranged and organised to cover the different fields (biochemistry, photography, cinematography, electronics, navigation, optics, acoustics, meteorology, geology, telegraphy, radio, television, astronomy, shipbuilding, aeronautics, industrial processes, etc.). Thus the section on gas illustrates the history of gas manufacture and distribution from the earliest days to the modern drilling platforms; the aeronautics gallery contains models and actual aircraft of different generations as well as hot-air balloons and other notable flying machines; and the special children's gallery has dioramas and models illustrating the development of transport and energy production. Of the museum's endless range of exhibits only a few can be selected to indicate the scope and interest of the collection: models of historic 18th and 19th c. machines, including those of Watt, Parsons and Diesel; Graham Bell's first telephone; Galileo's telescopes; Egyptian weights and measures of the 14th c. B.C.; models of Egyptian ships, Viking craft, Columbus's "Santa Maria" and Nelson's "Victory"; a model of Murdock's first gas-works; Stephenson's "Rocket" loco-

Science Museum: a 1909 Rolls-Royce

motive; the earliest X-ray apparatus; chemicals and their composition; apparatus used in atomic physics; electronic data-processing machines; Otto Lilienthal's first glider; models of space satellites (Vostock, Mercury, Gemini).
The Science Museum is also famed for its library (380,000 volumes).

*The Sir John Soane Museum   G3

The unusual feature of this museum, in the house which belonged to the celebrated architect and collector Sir John Soane, is that everything has been left as it was at the time of Soane's death in 1837, from the furniture and furnishings to the arrangement of the smallest trinkets. The general effect is perhaps a little untidy and overcrowded, but at the same time this gives the museum a particular charm of its own. Apart from this, the collection is well worth visiting in its own right.
The main rooms which should be seen are the entrance hall, dining room, dressing room and library; the Picture Room, with paintings by Hogarth, Turner, Callcott and others; the "Crypt" and "Sepulchral Chamber", with the sarcophagus of Seti I (father of Ramesses the Great), hewn from a single block of alabaster; the Dome, crowded with antiquities; the New Picture Room, with sculpture and paintings by Watteau and Canaletto; the breakfast room and a number of studies and work-rooms.

Address
13 Lincoln's Inn Fields, WC2

Underground station
Holborn

Opening times
Tues.–Sat. 10 a.m.–5 p.m.

Closed
1 Jan., Good Friday, 24–26 Dec.

Admission free

Soho

The district of Soho (from an old hunting cry), bounded on the W by Regent Street, on the N by Oxford Street, on the E by Charing Cross Road and on the S by Shaftesbury Avenue, is a part of London which means different things to different people.

For the businessman Soho is a good address. Its convenient central situation has led a wide range of businesses to establish themselves here – film companies, publishers, sound-recording studios, record companies, exporters and agencies of all kinds. During business hours the life of Soho is dominated by the comings and goings of those employed in these various activities.

Soho is also a Mecca for the gourmet, with its specialised food and delicatessen shops and its restaurants offering a wide range of international cuisines. Since the latter part of the 17th c., when thousands of Huguenot refugees from France settled here after the revocation of the Edict of Nantes in 1685, to be followed later by Italians, Swiss, Chinese, Indians and newcomers of many other nationalities, Soho has been an area much given to foreign cuisines – at first in the family but later also on a commercial basis, often in small restaurants consisting of no more than a single room. The original clientele of the Soho restaurants was made up of thrifty foreigners and poor students: it has now become fashionable to eat in Soho, and a meal in this quarter can sometimes be expensive.

Underground stations
Piccadilly Circus, Oxford Circus, Tottenham Court Road

▲ *Soho by night*
◀ *Sir John Soane's Museum*

Soho by day

Market in Soho

There are, however, still numbers of reasonably priced restaurants in Soho; and since they are open for lunch as well as dinner a meal in Soho can be combined with a stroll through the streets of this very characteristic quarter of London.

For many visitors, too, Soho is a world of dubious entertainments, clip joints, late night shows, sex shops and callgirls' flats. In this respect as in others Soho caters for every taste.

Somerset House   G3

Somerset House, now partly occupied by government offices (the Board of Inland Revenue) and also used for various exhibitions, was built by Sir William Chambers in 1777–86. The E wing (King's College, part of the University of London) and the W wing were added in the 19th c. Before their move to Burlington House the Royal Academy (see entry), Royal Society and Society of Antiquaries were housed here.

The main entrance is in the Strand, but the principal front, nearly 200 m (600 ft) long, faces the Thames. Before the construction of the Victoria Embankment the central arch of the ground floor arcade was a water gate. The best view of the building is to be had from the terrace on the S bank of the Thames, looking through the arches of Waterloo Bridge.

The finest rooms have recently been renovated and are open to the public when used for exhibitions. It is well worth while taking the opportunity of an exhibition to see these handsome apartments, which merit a visit in their own right.

Address
Strand, WC2

Underground station
Temple

Opening times
Open only during exhibitions

*Southwark Cathedral   J3

Southwark Cathedral – officially the Cathedral and Collegiate Church of St Saviour and St Mary Overy – is the mother church of the diocese of Southwark, which covers most of S London, and after Westminster Abbey is London's finest Gothic church. According to the traditional legend a nunnery was founded on this spot by a ferryman's daughter called Mary and was named after her St Mary of the Ferry (later corrupted into St Mary Overy). In the 9th c. the nunnery became a house of Augustinian canons. A large Norman church, of which some remains still survive, was built in 1106, and after this was destroyed by fire it was rebuilt in Gothic style in 1206. From this period date the lower part of the 55 m (165 ft) high tower (the tower itself is 15th c.), the crossing, the choir and the ambulatory. The nave, added in the 13th c., was rebuilt in 1469 and after a partial collapse in 1838 was re-erected by Sir Arthur Blomfield.

The Cathedral is entered by the SW door. To the left can be seen a length of 13th c. arcading. In front of this is the font.

At the W end of the N aisle are a number of interesting carved wooden bosses from the 15th c. roof. Among the subjects depicted are a pelican feeding her young on her own blood (a popular symbol of self-sacrifice); Judas Iscariot (wearing a kilt!) being devoured by the Devil; gluttony, represented by a man with a swollen face; and the figure of a liar, a man with a twisted tongue.

Address
London Bridge, SE1

Underground station
London Bridge

Opening times
7.30 a.m.–6 p.m.

Also in the N aisle is the 12th c. Norman doorway which gave access to the cloister. Under the sixth window is the tomb of the poet John Gower (1330–1408), who enjoyed the patronage of Richard II and Henry IV. Under the head of the life-size effigy are depicted his three books – "Speculum Meditantis" (in French), "Vox Clamantis" (in Latin) and "Confessio Amantis" (in English).

In the crossing is a brass chandelier of 1680, richly ornamented and of imposing size. Four massive 13th c. piers support the central tower.

The N transept, which preserves wall paintings of the Norman period, dates from the 13th c. It contains three interesting monuments:

A monument to Joyce Austin (d. 1626) by Nicholas Stone.

A monument to the quack doctor Lionel Lockyer (1672), whose wonder-working pills, made from sunbeams, earned him a great contemporary reputation.

The Blisse monument, with a fine bust of Richard Blisse (d. 1703) under a canopy.

Also in the N transept is the Harvard Chapel, originally the Chapel of St John the Evangelist, which was given its present name in 1907 after its restoration by Harvard University. It commemorates John Harvard, baptised in this church in 1607, who emigrated to America and became the benefactor of the world-famous university which bears his name.

The chapel is entered through two round-headed Norman arches (several times restored), and other Norman work can be seen to the left of the altar. Also to the left of the altar are the arms of Harvard University, presented to the cathedral by Harvard students; to the right are the arms of Emmanuel College, Cambridge, of which Harvard was a member.

An elegant pointed arch gives access to the choir ambulatory, which contains a number of interesting monuments:

The Trehearne monument, which shows John Trehearne, "gentleman porter" to and favourite of James I, and his family, all in contemporary costume. The inscription quaintly records the king's regret that Death could not be persuaded to leave him his servant.

The late 13th c. effigy of a knight, finely carved in oak – one of the few such effigies surviving from that period.

The tomb of Alderman Richard Humble, depicted with his two wives (early 17th c.).

The choir and retrochoir are among the oldest Gothic work in London. The choir itself was built about 1273. On the N side of the sanctuary are the bishop's throne and stalls for the suffragan bishops. The high altar dates from 1520, but its columns are 13th c.

Behind the high altar is the 13th c. retrochoir (restored on a number of occasions). On the N side is a 16th c. oak chest, a masterpiece of inlaid work and expressive carving.

At the E end of the retrochoir are four chapels: St Andrew's Chapel; St Christopher's Chapel; the Lady Chapel, a graceful example of the Early English style, built at the same time as the choir; and the Chapel of St Francis and St Elizabeth of Hungary.

In the S ambulatory is the tomb of Bishop Lancelot Andrewes (1626), one of the team of translators who produced the Authorised Version of the Bible.

Southwark Cathedral ▶

In the S transept (Gothic, *c.* 1310) are the arms and cardinal's hat of Henry Beaufort, Henry IV's half-brother and one of the most active and influential men of his day, whose niece, Joan Beaufort, was married to James I of Scotland in this church.

Speakers' Corner

See Marble Arch

Stock Exchange   J3

Address
Old Broad Street, EC2

Underground station
Bank

Buses
6, 8, 9, 11, 15, 21, 22, 23, 25, 43, 76

Opening times
Mon.–Fri. 9.45 a.m.–3.15 p.m.

The London Stock Exchange – the institution for the buying and selling of stocks and shares – is, in terms of business done, the largest in the world.

The Stock Exchange was founded in 1773. It is now housed in a large modern building completed between 1970 and 1973, with a 26-storey tower block, which replaced an earlier building erected in 1802.

The new building includes a viewing gallery from which visitors can watch the activity on the floor of the Exchange.

**Tate Gallery   G5

Address
Millbank, SW1

Underground station
Pimlico

Opening times
Mon.–Sat. 10 a.m.–5.50 p.m., Sun. 2–5.50 p.m.

Closed
1 Jan., Good Friday, 1st Mon. in May, 24–25 Dec.

Admission free

The Tate Gallery, one of London's largest art collections, was opened in 1897 in a classical-style building designed by Sidney R. J. Smith on Millbank, on the banks of the Thames. The gallery was built at the expense of Sir Henry Tate, a wealthy art collector, who presented his own collection to the nation as the basis of a national collection of significant British pictures from the 16th c. to the present day.

Since its foundation the gallery has been much enlarged – in 1910, 1926, 1937 and, most recently, 1979. It now consists of three main complexes – a national gallery of British art, a gallery of modern sculpture and a gallery of modern pictures by foreign artists.

In the national collection Turner, Blake, Kneller, Lely, Gainsborough, Hogarth, Reynolds, Wilson, Crome, Landseer and Constable are particularly well represented.

The collection of modern sculpture includes works by Rodin, Eric Gill, Maillol, Meštrović, Picasso, Epstein and Henry Moore.

The collection of pictures by foreign artists is particularly strong in the French Impressionists and Post-Impressionists (Cézanne, Degas, Gauguin, Manet, Monet, Sisley, Pissaro, H. Rousseau, Toulouse-Lautrec, Utrillo, Bonnard, Dufy, Chagall, Picasso, Rouault) and the Expressionists, Cubists and Surrealists.

Visitors who wish to study the collection in more detail will do well to purchase the current catalogue.

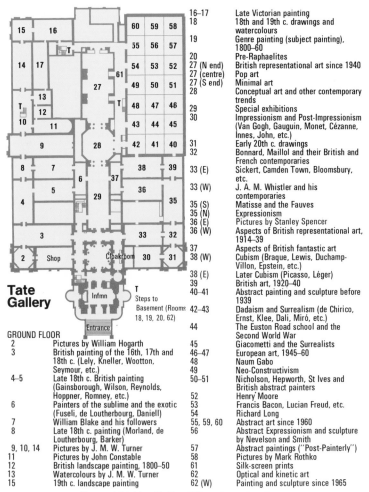

Tate Gallery

GROUND FLOOR

Rooms not listed (e.g. 21, 22 and 23) are at present empty

Temple   H3

The Temple is a quiet and secluded corner of London, an oasis of pleasant gardens and attractive Georgian buildings. Dickens caught its atmosphere in "Barnaby Rudge": "There are, still, worse places than the Temple, on a sultry day, for basking in the sun, or resting idly in the shade. There is yet a drowsiness in

Underground station
Temple

The Temple

its courts, and a dreamy dullness in its trees and gardens; and those who pace its lanes and squares may yet hear the echoes of their footsteps on the sounding stones, and read upon its gates in passing from the tumult of the Strand or Fleet Street, 'Who enters here leaves noise behind.' There is still the plash of falling water in fair Fountain Court . . .''

In the 12th and 13th c. the Temple was the headquarters in England of the order of Knights Templars, founded in Jerusalem in 1119. After the dissolution of the order in 1312 the property fell to the Crown; then in 1324 it was granted to the Knights of St John, who later in the century leased it to a group of professors of the common law. Since then the Temple has remained in the hands of the legal profession, housing two of the four Inns of Court which admit lawyers to practise as barristers in the English courts. It is in convenient proximity to the High Court of Justice on the N side of Fleet Street (see entry).

Barristers (who are entitled to plead in the higher courts of England but have no direct contact with their clients – in contrast to the other branch of the legal profession, the solicitors, who deal directly with the clients and ''instruct'' the barristers but are not themselves allowed to plead in the higher courts) must be trained in one of the four Inns of Court, which are in effect law schools with the exclusive right to admit candidates to practise as barristers. The two inns within the Temple are known as the Middle Temple and Inner Temple; the other two are Lincoln's Inn and Gray's Inn (see entries).

The Inns of Court were first established in the reign of Edward I, when the clergy had ceased to practise in the lawcourts and had been succeeded by professional lawyers. Each of the inns has a large complex of buildings, comprising legal chambers (offices) which are let to barristers and solicitors and extensive gardens as well as the actual teaching facilities (libraries, lecture rooms, dining halls, etc.), laid out around a number of courts.

In order to become a barrister a student must pass the examinations of one of the halls and must also fulfil the traditional requirement of dining in hall at least three times a term for twelve terms in all.

Each inn is governed by a committee of "benchers". All judges of the High Court automatically became benchers; other benchers are elected from among senior barristers (Q.C.s). The benchers of each inn are presided over by a treasurer, who is elected annually. Once every term the treasurer admits successful candidates to the bar on a ceremonial occasion known as Call Night.

The Temple is entered from Fleet Street through a handsome Wren gateway. To the W Of Middle Temple Lane is the Middle Temple, the members of which have included such notable figures as Sir Walter Raleigh, John Pym, Henry Fielding, Thomas Moore, Thomas de Quincey, W. M. Thackeray and R. B. Sheridan.

The Middle Temple Hall was built during the reign of Elizabeth I, in 1576, as a dining and assembly hall. After suffering severe bomb damage during the Second World War it was restored in the original style, and still preserves much of the original panelling, a carved screen in Elizabethan style, a magnificent double hammerbeam roof, armorial glass and a serving table made from the timbers of Drake's "Golden Hind". Judges and barristers still lunch in the hall, and here, too, the students dine during term.

Fountain Court, to the N, leads into Garden Court, from which there is a gate opening on to the Embankment.

On the E side of Middle Temple Lane is the entrance to Pump Court (1680), which gives access to the Inner Temple.

Inner Temple Hall, the dining and assembly hall of the Inner Temple, was destroyed by bombing in 1941 and rebuilt in 1952–5. It has a heated marble floor and stained-glass windows with the arms of former members of the inn. At the W end are a vaulted room and crypt dating from the 14th c.

Visitors are not admitted to the hall during vacations or on New Year's Day, Good Friday, Easter Monday or Christmas.

The Inner Temple Gardens, reaching down to the Thames, are not open to the public. In these gardens are still grown the white and red roses which according to tradition were plucked here at the beginning of the Wars of the Roses and became the emblems of the houses of York and Lancaster.

To the N of Inner Temple Hall is the Temple Church, which serves both inns. The original Norman church (1185), the "Round", circular in plan like the Church of the Holy Sepulchre in Jerusalem, had an oblong chancel in Early English style added in 1240. The church was renovated by Wren in 1682, and was carefully restored after suffering damage in the Second World War. It contains fine effigies of 12th and 13th c. Templar knights (restored).

The Temple Church has its own incumbent. It is used for the marriages of members of benchers' families, and memorial services are held here for deceased benchers.

Middle Temple Hall,
Middle Temple Lane

Opening times
Sat. 10 a.m.–4 p.m.,
Mon.–Fri. 10 a.m.–noon and
3–4.30 p.m.

Closed
1 Jan., Good Friday, Easter
Monday, 24–26 Dec.

Admission free

Inner Temple Hall

Opening times
Mon.–Fri. 10–11.30 a.m. and
2.30–4 p.m.

Admission free

Temple Church

Opening times
10 a.m.–5.30 p.m. (in winter
to 4.30 p.m.)

Closed
24–26 Dec.

Tower of London

The Tower of London is London's No. 1 tourist attraction and England's most historic building. It was a stronghold which was many times besieged but never taken; but it was also a

Address
Tower Hill, EC3M 4AB

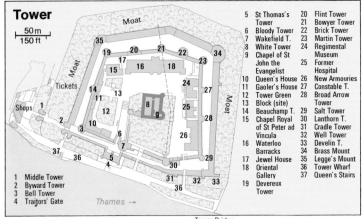

Tower

50 m		5	St Thomas's Tower
150 ft		6	Bloody Tower
		7	Wakefield T.
		8	White Tower
		9	Chapel of St John the Evangelist
		10	Queen's House
		11	Gaoler's House
		12	Tower Green
		13	Block (site)
		14	Beauchamp T.
		15	Chapel Royal of St Peter ad Vincula
		16	Waterloo Barracks
		17	Jewel House
		18	Oriental Gallery
		19	Devereux Tower
		20	Flint Tower
		21	Bowyer Tower
		22	Brick Tower
		23	Martin Tower
		24	Regimental Museum
		25	Former Hospital
		26	New Armouries
		27	Constable T.
		28	Broad Arrow Tower
		29	Salt Tower
		30	Lanthorn T.
		31	Cradle Tower
		32	Well Tower
		33	Develin T.
		34	Brass Mount
		35	Legge's Mount
		36	Tower Wharf
		37	Queen's Stairs

1 Middle Tower
2 Byward Tower
3 Bell Tower
4 Traitors' Gate

Tower Bridge

Underground station
Tower Hill

Opening times
Mar.–Oct., Mon.–Sat. 9.30 a.m.–5 p.m., Sun. 2–5 p.m.; Nov.–Feb., Mon.–Sat. 9.30 a.m.–4 p.m.

Closed
1 Jan., Good Friday, 1st Mon. in May, 24–26 Dec.

Admission charge

royal palace (until the time of James I), a prison (still used during the last war, when one of its inmates was Rudolf Hess), a mint (until the opening of the Royal Mint nearby in 1810), a treasure vault (still containing the crown jewels), an observatory (until the establishment of Greenwich Observatory (see entry) in 1675) and for five centuries (until 1834) a menagerie.

The Tower was built by William the Conqueror after the battle of Hastings to protect London, to overawe its citizens and to enable shipping on the Thames to be watched. The original Tower, built about 1078 and surrounded by a ring of walls with 13 towers, is now known as the White Tower. The fortress was enlarged and strengthened in the 12th c., and again in the 13th and 14th. It was restored in the 19th c.

The history of the Tower reflects the history of England. It has been the place of confinement of many historical personages, among them King David II of Scotland (1346–57), King John the Good of France (1356–60), King James I of Scotland (1406–7), Charles, Duke of Orleans (1415), Princess Elizabeth, later Queen Elizabeth I (1554), Sir Walter Raleigh (1592, 1603–16, 1618) and William Penn (1668–9). Many famous people, too, have been executed or murdered within its walls, including Henry VI (1471), the "Princes in the Tower" (Edward V and his brother the Duke of York, 1483), Sir Thomas More (1535), Henry VIII's queens Anne Boleyn (1536) and Catherine Howard (1542), Thomas Cromwell (1540), Jane Grey, the "Nine Days Queen" (1554), and the Duke of Monmouth (1685). The last executions carried out in the Tower took place during the Second World War, when a number of spies were shot here.

The history of the Tower is illustrated in a recently opened History Gallery.

The Tower, covering a roughly square area some 18 acres in extent, consists of an Outer Ward and an Inner Ward containing its historic buildings. The Outer Ward is surrounded by a wall with six towers and two bastions, probably built by Edward I in the 14th c., and is separated from the Inner Ward by a wall with 13 towers dating from the reign of Henry III.

The entrance to the Tower is at the SW corner, formerly the site of the Lion Tower, in which the royal menagerie was housed from the 14th c. until 1834.

(1) Just beyond the entrance is the Middle Tower, built in the reign of Edward I (1307) and restored in the 19th c. This tower was formerly accessible only by two drawbridges.

(2) Beyond this stands the Byward Tower (from "byword", password), also built in the reign of Edward I and restored in the 19th c. It contains guardrooms and the machinery for the portcullis, which can be seen in the upper rooms. A 14th c. wall painting of the Crucifixion was discovered here during restoration work in 1953.

(3) In the narrow Outer Ward between the two circuits of walls, to the left, is the Bell Tower, built by Richard I about 1190 but altered in the 19th c.

On the rampart running N from here to the Beauchamp Tower is Princess Elizabeth's Walk.

(4) Through the Traitors' Gate on the bank of the Thames prisoners were admitted to the Tower after being brought by boat from Westminster.

(5) Here, too, is St Thomas's Tower, built by Henry III in 1242, with a small chapel dedicated to St Thomas Becket.

(6) The Bloody Tower, built by Richard II, was in medieval times the only entrance to the Inner Ward. The name reflects the dark deeds, including the murder of the Princes in the Tower, which are associated with this tower.

Tower of London: a bird's-eye view

(7) Immediately adjoining is the massive Wakefield Tower, also built by Henry III. Henry VI, the last king of the house of Lancaster, is said to have been murdered in a vaulted room in this tower in 1471. The crown jewels were kept in the Wakefield Tower until 1968, when they were moved to a new strongroom in the Jewel House. The Great Hall, in which Anne Boleyn was tried, formerly adjoined the tower.

(8) In the centre of the Inner Ward is the White Tower, the original Norman stronghold, so called from the white Caen stone of which it was built. It now houses a collection of arms and armour. The tower was begun in 1078 for William the Conqueror by Gundulf, later bishop of Rochester, continued by William Rufus and completed by Ranulph Flambard, bishop of Durham, about 1100. Flambard himself was the first prisoner to be incarcerated in the Tower.

The White Tower is of four storeys, with walls up to 5 m (15 ft) thick. The small cupolas on the corner turrets were added in the 17th c. The exterior was restored by Wren.

A staircase on the N side leads into the interior, which has undergone little change and still gives an excellent impression of the structure of a Norman fortress.

The collection of arms and armour is displayed on three floors. On the first floor are hunting and sporting weapons from medieval times to the end of the 19th c. The Tournament Gallery contains arms and armour used in tournaments (15th–16th c.). On the second floor is a collection of European arms and armour from the early Middle Ages to the end of the 16th c. Finally on the fourth floor are arms and armour which belonged to Henry VIII and a gallery of 17th c. Stuart armour (including a suit of gilt armour which was worn by Charles I).

(9) Within the structure of the White Tower, occupying the height of two floors, is St John's Chapel, a well-preserved example of Norman church architecture (1080).

On the W side of the Inner Ward are the Queen's House, the Yeoman Gaoler's House, the tree-planted area known as Tower Green, the site of the execution block, the Beauchamp Tower and the chapel of St Peter ad Vincula.

(10) The Queen's House is an attractive half-timbered Tudor house in which Anne Boleyn spent her last days before execution. Now the residence of the Governor of the Tower, it is not open to the public.

(11) Adjoining is the Yeoman Gaoler's House, a 17th c. house in which Rudolf Hess was confined after his flight from Germany to Scotland in 1941. On ceremonial occasions the Yeoman Gaoler still wears his traditional uniform and carries his executioner's axe.

(12) In front of these buildings is Tower Green.

(13) On Tower Green is a small square formation of granite setts marking the site of the execution block on which condemned prisoners were beheaded with an axe. Exceptionally, Anne Boleyn was beheaded with a sword.

(14) The Beauchamp Tower is named after Thomas Beauchamp, Earl of Warwick, who was imprisoned here in the reign of Richard II (1397–9). This three-storey semicircular tower was built about 1300 and was principally used as a prison. On the walls are inscriptions (now numbered) carved by the prisoners.

Entrance to the Tower ▶

(15) The Chapel Royal of St Peter ad Vincula takes its name from the day on which it was consecrated, the festival of St Peter in Chains. Probably built about 1100, it was altered in the 13th c., rebuilt after a fire in 1512 and thereafter several times renovated and restored. Here are buried many of those executed in the Tower.

The whole of the N side of the Inner Ward is occupied by the Waterloo Barracks.

(16) The Waterloo Barracks were built in 1845 to house the Royal Fusiliers, who occupied them until 1962. They now contain a collection of arms and armour, the Oriental Gallery and the Jewel House.

Crown Jewels

(17) The entrance to the Jewel House is at the left-hand end of the barrack buildings. This is a new strongroom under the barracks in which the Crown Jewels have been kept since 1968.

Most of the very valuable Crown Jewels date from after 1660, since the older regalia were sold or melted down during the Commonwealth. Particularly notable items in this unique collection are the following:

St Edward's Crown, of pure gold, made for the coronation of Charles II and still used in the crowning of British sovereigns.

The Imperial State Crown, set with over 3000 diamonds and other precious stones, including a huge ruby presented to the Black Prince by Pedro the Cruel of Castile in 1369 and one of the two "Stars of Africa" cut from the Cullinan Diamond, the largest ever found. This crown was made for the coronation of Queen Victoria (1838), and is worn at the state opening of Parliament and on other state occasions.

The Imperial Indian Crown (made in 1911), set with over 6000 diamonds and an emerald of over 34 carats.

Queen Elizabeth's Crown, with the famous 108-carat Koh-i-Noor diamond. The crown was made for George VI's queen, now Queen Elizabeth the Queen Mother.

The Royal Sceptre, with the second "Star of Africa", the largest cut diamond in the world (530 carats).

(18) The Oriental Gallery displays Oriental arms and armour.

Along the N wall of the Inner Ward are a series of towers:

(19) Devereux Tower.

(20) Flint Tower.

(21) Bowyer Tower, with a torture chamber containing a collection of old instruments of torture and execution.

(22) Brick Tower.

(23) Martin Tower.

On the E side of the Inner Ward are:

(24) the Regimental Museum of the Royal Fusiliers, with regimental relics and trophies.

(25) the former Hospital.

(26) the New Armouries.

The names of the towers on the E wall of the Inner Ward are:

(27) Constable Tower.

(28) Broad Arrow Tower.

(29) Salt Tower.

(30) Lanthorn Tower, at the SE corner of the walls.

On the S side of the outer circuit of walls are three other towers:

(31) the Cradle Tower, a 14th c. water tower.

(32) the Well Tower, with vaulting dating from the reign of Henry III.

(33) the Develin Tower.

The Crown Jewels

The outer walls are reinforced by two bastions built by Henry VIII:
(34) Brass Mount, at the NE corner.
(35) Legge's Mount, at the NW corner.
Between the Cradle Tower and Well Tower is an opening leading to the Tower Wharf, originally constructed in 1228.
(36) On Tower Wharf salutes are fired on royal occasions such as the accession and coronation of a sovereign or the birth of a prince or princess. The firing of such salutes is a privilege of the Honourable Artillery Company, Britain's oldest military unit, originally formed by Henry VIII in 1537 as the Fraternity of St George, which still provides the guard of honour on royal visits to the City.
(37) From the wharf the Queen's Stairs descend to the Thames. The Tower is guarded by the Yeomen Warders, a body of 40 ex-soldiers who still wear their traditional Tudor uniform and are referred to by their popular name of "Beefeaters". They are often confused with the Yeoman of the Guard (see St James's Palace).
Among their duties is the ceremonial closing of the gates each evening, the 700-year-old Ceremony of the Keys, in which the Chief Warder presents the keys of the Tower to the Resident Governor.
While the Yeomen Warders are responsible for the safety of the Tower, the six ravens which are kept within the precincts have an even wider responsibility for the protection of the whole British Commonwealth, which – legend has it – will fall if they ever leave the Tower.

Ceremony of the Keys
For permission to attend, apply in writing to the Resident Governor, Tower of London, EC3N 4AB

Admission 9.35 p.m. at main entrance

Tower Bridge

*Tower Bridge K3

Tower Bridge, opened in 1894, is one of London's best known landmarks, with its two neo-Gothic towers rising 65 m (200 ft) above the river, with the walkway open to the public.

The two heavy bascules or drawbridges bearing the carriageway can be raised in a minute and a half to allow large ships to pass through (a rare occurrence nowadays, since cargo vessels now moor farther downstream). Since 1975 they have been raised by electric power. There is also a museum housing the older hydraulic machinery which is still maintained in working order so as to be available in case of emergency.

Address
Whitechapel, EC1

Underground station
Tower Hill

Opening times
Nov.–Mar, 10 a.m.–
4.45 p.m., Apr.–Oct.,
10 a.m.–6.30 p.m.

Admission charge

*Trafalgar Square and Nelson's Column G3

Nelson's Column ranks with Big Ben and Tower Bridge (see entry) as one of the great London landmarks, and Trafalgar Square is one of the city's most popular meeting-places for tourists from all over the world.

The square, the name of which commemorates Nelson's victory over a French and Spanish fleet at Trafalgar in 1805, was laid out between 1829 and 1851 by Sir Charles Barry. Its central feature is the 56 m (185 ft) high Nelson Monument, or Nelson's Column, by William Railton (1840–3), constructed of granite from Devon. From the summit of the column a statue of Nelson 9 m (27 ft) high, looks down on the busy activity of Trafalgar Square, with its fountains (designed by Sir Edward Lutyens and erected in 1948), its pigeons, its swarming humanity and its swirling traffic.

On the base of the monument are four bronze reliefs depicting Nelson's victories at Cape St Vincent, the Nile, Copenhagen and Trafalgar. The bronze lions at the four corners were modelled by Sir Edwin Landseer (1868).

Under the balustrade on the N side of the square, in front of the National Gallery (see entry), the Imperial standards of length (1 inch, 1 foot, 2 feet, 1 yard, 1 chain and 100 feet) are let into the stone.

Underground station
Charing Cross

**Victoria and Albert Museum D4

The Victoria and Albert Museum is part of the great complex of museums in South Kensington (the others being the Natural History Museum, the Science Museum and the Geological Museum – see entries). The idea of the "V and A" came from Prince Albert, and the museum was originally financed from the profits of the Great Exhibition of 1851. The foundation stone of the present building was laid by Queen Victoria in 1899, and it was formally opened by Edward VII in 1909 as the national museum of fine and applied arts. With its extensive collections of material from many countries and many periods it is one of the world's great art museums.

◀ *Trafalgar Square and Nelson's Column*

Address
Cromwell Road, South
Kensington, SW7

Underground station
South Kensington

Opening times
Mon.–Thurs. and Sat.
10 a.m.–5.50 p.m., Sun.
2.30–5.50 p.m.

Closed
1 Jan., 1st Mon. in May, 24–
26 Dec.

Admission free

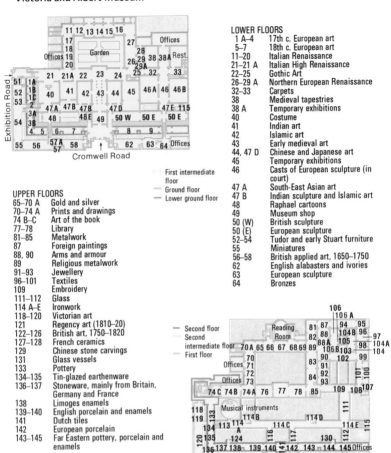

Victoria and Albert Museum

The exhibits are arranged in two groups – the Primary Collections, in which masterpieces in every field of art are brought together by style, period and country of origin, and the Study Collections, in which the objects are grouped according to the material used (wood, metal, ceramics, textiles, etc.). Every department of the museum contains a great range of treasures – whether in the field of Byzantine and early medieval art, ceramics and porcelain, prints and drawings, metalwork or musical instruments. The museum has a valuable collection of paintings, including many works by Constable, but it is notable

Victoria and Albert Museum ▶

also for its collection of British miniatures and watercolours and for the cartoons done by Raphael for Pope Leo X in 1516. The textile department is of great interest, but so, too, are the departments of woodcarving, alabasters and ivories. The furniture is displayed in a series of rooms completely furnished in period style. The collections of Islamic and Far Eastern art are of notable quality.

With such a wealth of valuable and interesting material, it is not possible within the compass of this guide to list even a selection of the finest exhibits. The best plan – since it is manifestly impossible to get round the whole museum in a single visit – is to study the plans on p. 132 and decide which items or sections you particularly want to see. If you want to study some particular field in more detail it is well worth while purchasing the current catalogue of the museum, which will also give information about new acquisitions or rearrangements of the exhibits.

For ease of reference the rooms are listed in numerical order. It should be observed, however, that adjoining rooms may not have adjoining numbers, so that the various rooms cannot be visited in regular numerical sequence.

---

*Wallace Collection   E3

Address
Hertford House, Manchester Square, W1

Underground stations
Baker Street, Bond Street

Opening times
Mon.–Sat. 10 a.m.–5 p.m., Sun. 2–5 p.m.

Closed
1 Jan., Good Friday, 1st Mon. in May, 24–26 Dec.

Admission free

The Wallace Collection, one of the most valuable art collections ever presented to the nation by a private person, is housed in a mansion built for the Duke of Manchester in 1776–88 which, in spite of much subsequent alteration, still gives an excellent impression of the appearance of a great town house of the period.

The basis of the collection was laid by the third and fourth Marquesses of Hertford. The son of the fourth Marquess, Sir Richard Wallace, added to the collection, which was bequeathed to the nation by his widow and opened to the public in 1900. Since then nothing has been changed, for it was a condition of the bequest that the collection should be kept intact, "unmixed with other objects of art".

The collection contains an extraordinarily wide range of works of the highest quality in many different genres – French pictures, porcelain and furniture of the 17th and 18th c.; European and Oriental arms and armour; Renaissance terracottas, jewellery, bronzes and goldsmiths' work; pictures by British, Flemish, Spanish and Italian masters.

The collection is displayed in 22 rooms on the ground and upper floors, in the following order:

Louis XVI furniture; chairs covered with Beauvais tapestry (designs by Casanova).

Italian majolica of the Renaissance period, including Giorgio Andreoli's "Bath of the Maidens"; 15th and 17th c. bronzes.

European arms and armour of the 15th c. onwards (temporarily closed).

European arms and armour, Oriental arms and armour and paintings of Oriental subjects by French artists (temporarily closed).

Venetian paintings by Canaletto, Guardi and others.

Terracottas, furniture and paintings by Cima, Luini, Andrea del Sarto, Sassoferrato, Foppa, Titian and others.

Apsley House (Wellington Museum)

Spanish and Italian masters of the 17th c.
Sèvres porcelain, furniture and clocks of the time of Louis XV and XVI and pictures by Canaletto and Guardi.
17th c. Dutch and Flemish masters, including Rubens ("Christ on the Cross"), Rembrandt, A. van der Neer, van Noort, Cornelis de Vos, Brouwer, Metsu, van Ostade, Jan Steen and Terborch.
17th c. Dutch landscapes and seascapes (Cuyp, van Ostade, van Ruisdael, van de Velde, etc.).
Works by Rembrandt, Frans Hals, van Dyck, Rubens, Titian, Velázquez, Murillo, Gainsborough, Reynolds, Watteau, etc.
19th c. French painting (Corot, Delacroix, Géricault, etc.).
18th c. French art (Watteau, Lancret, Boucher, Fragonard, Nattier); three secretaires which belonged to Marie Antoinette.
Chest of drawers which belonged to Marie Antoinette; pictures by Boucher.
French furniture, including a writing-table once the property of Catherine the Great.
Sèvres porcelain, miniatures, still-lifes by Desportes.

*Wellington Museum

E4

The Wellington Museum is in Apsley House, for many years the town house of the first Duke of Wellington (1769–1852). Apsley House was built by Robert Adam between 1771 and 1778 for Baron Apsley, later Earl Bathurst, and was bought by Wellington after his victory at Waterloo. The Duke made many changes to the house: originally of red brick, it was refaced with Bath stone in 1828–9 by Benjamin Wyatt, who also added the Corinthian portico and the famous Waterloo Gallery in which the Waterloo Banquet was held annually until the Duke's

Address
Apsley House, 149
Piccadilly, Hyde Park
Corner, W1

Underground station
Hyde Park Corner

Wellington Museum: the Waterloo Gallery

Opening times
Tues.–Thurs. and Sat. 10 a.m.–6 p.m., Sun. 2.30–6 p.m.

Closed
Bank Holidays

Admission free

death. In 1947 Apsley House was presented to the nation by the seventh Duke of Wellington, and in 1952 it was opened to the public as the Wellington Museum.

The house contains numerous mementoes of the Iron Duke. In the entrance hall are a marble bust of Wellington and two notable pictures by Turner ("Tapping the Furnace") and Landseer ("A Dialogue at Waterloo").

In the China Room is part of the service of porcelain presented to the Duke by Frederick William III of Prussia after the Battle of Waterloo.

In the Piccadilly Drawing Room on the first floor are a fine "Agony in the Garden" by Correggio and three works by Jan Bruegel the Elder.

Among the paintings captured by the Duke from Joseph Bonaparte after the battle of Vitoria (1813) and later presented to him by the king of Spain are works by Velázquez, Rubens, Murillo and Sassoferrato.

**Westminster Abbey

****Westminster Abbey**   G4

Address
Broad Sanctuary, SW1

Underground stations
Westminster, St James's Park

Westminster Abbey – officially the Collegiate Church of St Peter in Westminster – was founded by Edward the Confessor in 1065 as his place of interment, and from his burial (1066) until that of George II (1760) most English and British sovereigns were buried here, as well as numerous prominent national figures.

Westminster Abbey

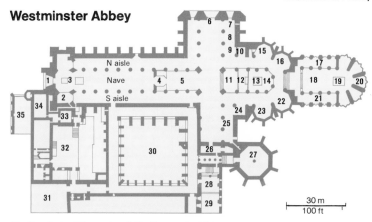

Collegiate Church of St Peter in Westminster

1 West doorway
2 St George's Chapel
3 Tomb of Unknown Warrior and Churchill memorial
4 Organ loft
5 Choir
6 North doorway
7 St Andrew's Chapel
8 St Michael's Chapel
9 Chapel of St John the Evangelist
10 Islip Chapel
11 Sanctuary

12 High altar
13 St Edward's Chapel
14 Henry V's Chantry Chapel
15 Chapel of St John the Baptist
16 St Paul's Chapel
17 Tomb of Elizabeth I
18 Henry VII's Chapel
19 Tomb of Henry VII
20 RAF Chapel (Battle of Britain Memorial Window)
21 Tomb of Mary Queen of Scots
22 St Nicholas's Chapel
23 St Edmund's Chapel

24 St Benedict's Chapel
25 Poets' Corner
26 St Faith's Chapel
27 Chapter House
28 Chapel of the Pyx
29 Undercroft Museum
30 Cloisters
31 Dean's Yard
32 Deanery
33 Jericho Parlour
34 Jerusalem Chamber
35 Bookshop

Opening times
8 a.m.–6 p.m., Wed. 8 a.m.–8 p.m.

Since 1066, when William the Conqueror was crowned here, Westminster Abbey has been the place of coronation of every subsequent sovereign except Edward V and Edward VIII, as well as the scene of many royal weddings.

Edward the Confessor's Norman church was rebuilt by Henry III in a style influenced by French Gothic, but only the nave was completed during his reign. After suffering destruction in a fire (1298), parts of the abbey were rebuilt by Henry Yevele in 1388 on the basis of the 13th c. plans. The vaulting of the nave was completed by Abbot Islip in 1506. The Gothic-style W front with its two towers was the work of Nicholas Hawksmoor, a pupil of Wren (1735–40).

A masterpiece of Gothic architecture, Westminster Abbey has the highest Gothic nave in England (34 m – 102 ft).

(1) The Abbey is entered by the W door.

(2) To the right is St George's Chapel, formerly the baptistery, which is dedicated to those who fell in the First World War.

(3) Immediately ahead, on the floor of the nave, is the Tomb of the Unknown Warrior, and beyond this is a memorial stone commemorating Sir Winston Churchill (1874–1965). Other slabs in the nave mark the graves of the architects Sir Charles Barry, Sir George Gilbert Scott, G. E. Street and J. L. Pearson; David Livingstone, the African missionary and explorer (d.

1873); the engineers Robert Stephenson (d. 1859) and Thomas Telford (d. 1834); Lord Clyde, Lord Lawrence and Sir James Outram, who distinguished themselves during the Indian Mutiny; and the statesmen Bonar Law (d. 1923) and Neville Chamberlain (d. 1940).

(4) Organ loft, in the nave.

(5) The choir, which occupies the same position as the choir of Edward the Confessor's earlier church.

Royal Chapels

(6) Then past the N entrance to the royal chapels.

(7) St Andrew's Chapel.

Opening times
Mon.–Fri. 9.20 a.m.–
4.45 p.m. (last admissions
4 p.m.), Sat. 9.20 a.m.–
2.45 p.m. (last admissions
2 p.m.), and 3.45–5.45 p.m.
(last admission 5 p.m.)

(8) St Michael's Chapel.

(9) Chapel of St John the Evangelist.

(10) Islip Chapel, a two-storey structure. In the lower part is the tomb of Abbot Islip (d. 1532), who completed the nave of the Abbey.

(11) In front of the high altar is the Sanctuary, in which are the three finest medieval tombs in the Abbey. This is where the coronation ceremony takes place.

Admission charge

Opposite the tombs, on the S side of the sanctuary, are oak sedilia (seats for the officiating clergy), probably over tombs from the earlier church.

(12) On the high altar (by Sir George Gilbert Scott, 1867) are a glass mosaic of the Last Supper by Salviati and fine sculptured figures.

(13) St Edward's Chapel is built over the apse of the older church. In the centre is the shrine of Edward the Confessor, for many years a place of pilgrimage.

On the N side of the chapel is the marble tomb of Henry III (d. 1272), which, like the shrine, was made by Peter of Rome. Beside it is the tomb of Henry's daughter-in-law Eleanor of Castile, wife of Edward I. In this chapel, too, is the oak Coronation Chair, which is moved into the sanctuary for the coronation ceremony. Under the seat is the Stone of Scone, the ancient coronation seat of the kings of Scotland, which was carried off by Edward I. Its presence in the Coronation Chair is intended to symbolise the union of the crowns of England and Scotland.

On the S side of the chapel are the tombs of Richard II and his first wife Anne of Bohemia, the elaborate tomb of Edward III and the black marble tomb of Edward's queen Philippa of Hainault (d. 1369), with an effigy of white marble.

(14) Henry V's Chantry Chapel (15th c.).

(15) To the N of the high altar is the Chapel of St John the Baptist, in the centre of which is the large marble tomb of Thomas Cecil, Earl of Exeter (d. 1623), with an effigy of his first wife.

(16) Next to this is the Chapel of St Paul, with the tombs of Lord Bouchier, Henry V's standard-bearer, and Lord Cottington, Charles I's chancellor of the exchequer.

A few yards away is Henry VII's Chapel, a magnificent structure which is almost a church in itself. It was built in 1503–19 by Robert Vertue, Henry's master mason. This is the chapel of the Order of the Bath (originally founded in 1399).

(17) In the N aisle is the elaborately decorated tomb of Elizabeth I, with a marble effigy of the queen.

(18) Henry VII's Chapel itself is a superb example of Perpendicular architecture, with a profusion of rich sculptured

Westminster Abbey ▶

The marble Shrine of Edward the Confessor

decoration and beautiful fan vaulting. Under the altar is the grave of Edward VI (d. 1553).

(19) Behind the altar lies the tomb of Henry VII and his queen, Elizabeth of York (d. 1502), by the Florentine sculptor Torrigiani. Notable features of the tomb are the stalactitic canopy and the very beautiful bronze grille.

(20) One of the smaller chapels is now the Royal Air Force Chapel, with the Battle of Britain Memorial Window.

(21) Among the many interesting tombs in the S aisle of the chapel is that of Mary Queen of Scots, executed in 1587 on the orders of Elizabeth I.

(22) Chapel of St Nicholas. In the centre of the chapel is the marble tomb of Sir George Villiers (d. 1606) and his wife. Another notable tomb is that of Elizabeth, Duchess of Northumberland (d. 1676), a masterpiece by Robert Adam and Nicholas Read.

(23) Chapel of St Edmund. Outstanding among the many tombs in this chapel is that of William of Valence (d. 1296), half-brother to Henry III; the effigy is covered with gilded copper plates and decorated with Limoges enamel.

(24) Chapel of St Benedict, with the alabaster tomb of Simon Langham (d. 1376), abbot of Westminster and later archbishop of Canterbury.

(25) On the E side of the S transept is "Poets' Corner". Notable among the numerous monuments are busts of John Dryden (d. 1700) and Henry Wadsworth Longfellow (d. 1882), the marble tomb of Geoffrey Chaucer (d. 1400) and the tombs of Robert Browning (d. 1889) and Lord Tennyson (d. 1892).

(26) At the S end of the transept is the entrance to St Faith's Chapel, with two 16th c. Brussels tapestries.

(27) The fine Chapter House has been called "the cradle of all free parliaments", having been the meeting-place of the king's Great Council in 1257 and of Parliament from the mid-14th to the mid-16th c.

It is an octagonal chamber 20 m (60 ft) across, probably built by Henry of Reims (1245–55). The vaulting is supported on a single pier of clustered shafts (a copy of the original pier by Sir George Gilbert Scott, set up during restoration of the Chapter House in 1866). Other notable features are the well-preserved 13th c. pavement (for the protection of which visitors are provided with overshoes), the ornamental tracery of the six windows and the circular tympanum of the doorway, with figures of Christ in Majesty, the Virgin and angels (13th c.).

(28) The Chapel of the Pyx, originally a sacristy in Edward the Confessor's church, contains the oldest altar in the Abbey. It later became a royal treasury, in which was kept the "pyx", a chest containing the trial-plates of gold and silver used in the annual test of the coinage.

(29) The Norman Undercroft, part of Edward the Confessor's church, now houses the Abbey Museum, with old seals and charters, 14th and 15th c. chests, architectural fragments and the coronation chair of Mary II.

(30) The Cloisters are very attractive. The NE part dates from the mid-13th c.

(31) Dean's Yard and College Garden, said to be the oldest in England.

(32) Deanery.

(33) Jericho Parlour.

(34) Jerusalem Chamber, in which Henry IV died in 1413. It is now the chapter-room. (32, 33 and 34 are not open to the public.)

(35) Bookshop.

Chapter House

Opening times
Apr.–Sept., Mon.–Sat. 10.30 a.m.–6.30 p.m.; Oct.–Mar., Mon.–Sat. 10.30 a.m.– 4 p.m.

Closed
Daily noon–1 p.m.; Sun.; 1–2 Jan., Good Friday, 24–25 Dec.

Admission charge

Norman Undercroft

Opening times
Mon.–Fri. 9.15 a.m.–5 p.m. (last admissions 4.30 p.m.); Sat. 9.15 a.m.–5.30 p.m. (last admissions 5 p.m.); Sun. (Apr.–Sept.) 9.15 a.m.–5.30 p.m.

Closed
Good Friday, 1st Mon. in May, 25 Dec.

---

*Westminster Cathedral

F4

Westminster Cathedral, seat of the archbishop of Westminster, is the most important Roman Catholic cathedral in Britain, rivalled in size only by the Cathedral of Christ the King in Liverpool. Built in 1895–1903, it is a red-brick building in Byzantine style on a basilican plan, crowned by four domes.

The cathedral is usually entered by the NW doorway, to the left of which is the lift up the 94 m (284 ft) high campanile, St Edward's Tower. From the top of the tower there are extensive views over London.

(The tower is open to visitors from 10.30 a.m. to 5.30 p.m. April to October, from 10.30 a.m. to dusk during the rest of the year.) Near the entrance are two columns of red Norwegian granite, the colour symbolising the Precious Blood of Christ, to which the cathedral is dedicated. By the left-hand column is a bronze figure of St Peter, a copy of the famous statue in St Peter's Rome.

The nave is the widest in England (52 m – 150 ft, including the aisles). The decorative scheme is not yet complete, but even in its present state it is immensely impressive (variegated marbles on the lower parts of the walls, mosaics on the upper parts and

Address
Ashley Place, SW1

Underground station
Victoria

Opening times
7 a.m.–8 p.m. (25–26 Dec. 7 a.m.–4.30 p.m.)

the domes). On the main piers are Stations of the Cross carved by Eric Gill. The galleries over the aisles are borne on marble columns from the quarries which also supplied marble for St Sophia in Istanbul. The capitals, all different, are of white Carrara marble. The great cross which hangs from the arch at the E end of the nave is 10 m (30 ft) long, with painted figures of Christ and (on the back) the Mater Dolorosa.

Going along the N aisle, we come first to the Chapel of the Holy Souls, with beautiful mosaics of Old and New Testament scenes.

Next to this is St George's Chapel, with a figure of the saint. It contains the tomb of John Southwark, the "parish priest of Westminster", who was hanged at Tyburn in 1654.

The third chapel is the Chapel of St Joseph, with the tomb of Cardinal Hinsley (d. 1943) and beautiful marble mosaics.

In the N transept are a beautiful mosaic of Joan of Arc and the Chapel of St Thomas of Canterbury or Vaughan Chantry, with a fine statue of Cardinal Vaughan, who presided over the building of the cathedral. The little Chapel of the Sacred Heart and St Michael is decorated with Greek and Carrara marble.

Next comes the Chapel of the Blessed Sacrament, with ornate mosaic decoration (by Boris Anrep).

The high altar, in the sanctuary, has a marble canopy borne on columns. To the right of the sanctuary is the Lady Chapel, the first of the chapels to be completed, which is also decorated with very fine mosaics.

Steps lead down to the crypt (St Peter's Chapel), which contains a collection of treasured relics (including a mitre which belonged to St Thomas Becket) and fragments of the True Cross.

Adjoining is the small Chapel of St Edmund, with the tombs of bishops and cardinals.

Continuing round the nave, we come to the very fine white marble pulpit.

In the S aisle is the Chapel of St Paul, with a fine mosaic pavement based on a design by the Cosmati.

The Chapel of St Andrew and the Saints of Scotland has bas-relief figures of SS. Andrew, Ninian, Columba, Margaret and Bride.

Next comes the Chapel of St Patrick and the Saints of Ireland, decorated with Irish marble. In the niches are the badges of Irish regiments which fought in the First World War, and beside the altar is a casket containing the roll of honour of the 50,000 Irishmen who fell in the war. The marble pavement is in the form of a Celtic cross.

The adjoining Chapel of SS. Gregory and Augustine is notable for the altar mosaics depicting the conversion of England.

At the SW corner of the cathedral is the Baptistery, with an altar commemorating members of the Canadian Air Force who fell in the Second World War.

Westminster School

Westminster, one of the country's leading public schools, first appears in the records in 1339 as a monastic school, but was

Address
Dean's Yard, SW1

◀ *Westminster Cathedral: the nave*

Whitehall

Underground stations
Westminster, St James's
Park

Opening times
During school holidays
Mon.–Sat. noon–6 p.m.;
otherwise on written
application to Bursar,
Westminster School

re-founded by Elizabeth I in 1560. The College Hall, formerly
the abbey refectory and still a dining hall, contains tables which
are said to be made from timber recovered from ships of the
Spanish Armada. On the door are carved the names of former
pupils.
Every year at Christmas the school puts on a performance of a
Latin play in the original. Another annual event is the pancake-
tossing ceremony on Shrove Tuesday, a practice of unknown
origin which is believed to have started in the 18th c. One boy
from each form competes, and the boy who gets the largest
piece of pancake is presented with a guinea by the Dean of
Westminster.

Whitehall   G3/4

Underground stations
Westminster, Embankment,
Charing Cross

Whitehall, which preserves the memory of the old palace of that
name (see Banqueting House), is now synonymous with the
central government of the country and the civil service.
Coming from Trafalgar Square (see entry), we see on the right
the Admiralty, the older part of which was built by Thomas
Ripley in 1723–6, while the domed building to the rear was
added between 1895 and 1907. Beyond this is Horse Guards
(see entry).
On the opposite (W) side of the street is the Ministry of
Defence (the old War Office), followed by the Banqueting
House (see entry) and Gwydyr House, a handsome Georgian
building erected by John Marquand in 1772.

Government buildings in Whitehall

On the E side, beyond Horse Guards, are Dover House, occupied by the Scottish Office, and the old Treasury building, now housing the Cabinet Office. Opposite is a huge modern complex of government offices.

Beyond the little cul-de-sac with the famous name of Downing Street and the Cenotaph (see entries) is the section of Whitehall which bears the name of Parliament Street. Here, on the right, there are further large government offices – the Foreign and Commonwealth Office, the Home Office and the Treasury.

**Windsor Castle

With its old half-timbered houses and 17th and 18th c. inns, its cobbled streets and narrow lanes, the little town of Windsor, lying 35 km (22 miles) W of London on the S bank of the Thames, has still something of the picturesqueness of a medieval town.

Windsor Castle, on a chalk cliff above the Thames, has been for 900 years the summer residence of the royal family, one of the finest royal residences in the world and the largest castle which is still inhabited. When the Queen is at Windsor the royal standard flies from the Round Tower, and the State Apartments are then closed to the public; but the Lower Ward, the North Terrace, the Round Tower, St George's Chapel, the Albert Memorial Chapel, part of the East Terrace and the Curfew Tower are open throughout the year.

Address
Windsor, Berks

British Rail station
Windsor

Distance
35 km (22 miles) W of London (M4)

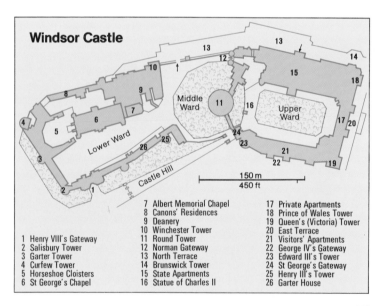

Windsor Castle

150 m
450 ft

1 Henry VIII's Gateway
2 Salisbury Tower
3 Garter Tower
4 Curfew Tower
5 Horseshoe Cloisters
6 St George's Chapel
7 Albert Memorial Chapel
8 Canons' Residences
9 Deanery
10 Winchester Tower
11 Round Tower
12 Norman Gateway
13 North Terrace
14 Brunswick Tower
15 State Apartments
16 Statue of Charles II
17 Private Apartments
18 Prince of Wales Tower
19 Queen's (Victoria) Tower
20 East Terrace
21 Visitors' Apartments
22 George IV's Gateway
23 Edward III's Tower
24 St George's Gateway
25 Henry III's Tower
26 Garter House

Windsor Castle: the largest inhabited castle in the world

William the Conqueror built a timber castle here about 1078, when the Tower of London was also being built, but of this structure nothing now survives. The first stone buildings were erected by Henry I about 1110; Henry II replaced the timber palisade with a stone wall reinforced by square towers; and Henry III built further defensive works, including the Curfew Tower. The castle was enlarged and strengthened by Edward III, who built the Round Tower; and the North Terrace was constructed in the reign of Elizabeth I. The picturesque old stronghold was converted into a comfortable residence in the reign of Charles II, but until comparatively recent times little use was made of it.

The senior English order of chivalry, the Order of the Garter, was established by Edward III at Windsor in 1348.

The vast complex of buildings which make up the castle is laid out around two courtyards, the Upper and the Lower Wards, with the Round Tower rising between the two. The State Apartments are on the N side of the Upper Ward; St George's Chapel, with two adjoining cloisters, is in the centre of the Lower Ward.

(1) The castle is entered by Henry VIII's Gateway, a monumental entrance in Tudor style.

The W end of the castle was defended by three towers:

(2) Salisbury Tower.

(3) Garter Tower.

(4) Curfew Tower, built in 1227, which incorporates some of the oldest masonry in the castle. The front and the roof were rebuilt in 1863. Within the tower is part of a 13th c. dungeon, with the beginning of an escape tunnel which was frustrated by the thickness of the walls.

(5) Straight ahead from the gateway are the Horseshoe Cloisters (restored 1871).

(6) Immediately E of the Horseshoe Cloisters is St George's Chapel, dedicated to the patron saint of the Order of the Garter. The chapel, a fine example of late Perpendicular architecture, was begun by Edward IV in 1477 and completed by Henry VIII. The N and S sides are decorated with pinnacles bearing the heraldic "royal beasts" of York and Lancaster. The W end has a large window with 16th c. stained glass.

The interior is notable for the fine lierne vaulting of the nave (1509) and the fan vaulting of the choir (1506) and for the choir-stalls, in local oak, carved with scenes from the life of St George and the crests of Knights of the Garter. In the choir are the tombs of Henry VIII, Jane Seymour and Charles I. (Most other sovereigns were buried in the Royal Tomb House beneath the Albert Memorial Chapel, originally built in 1240 and altered in the reign of Queen Victoria.)

(7) To the E of St George's Chapel is the Albert Memorial Chapel, built by Henry VII as a burial-place for Henry VI but left unfinished by him and completed by Cardinal Wolsey. Queen Victoria had it converted into a memorial chapel for Prince Albert. Its most notable features are the monument commemorating Prince Albert and the tomb of the Duke of Clarence, elder son of Edward VII.

(8) Behind St George's Chapel, against the N wall of the Lower Ward, are the Canons' Residences and Canons' Cloister.

(9) Between St George's Chapel and the Albert Memorial Chapel is a passage leading through the picturesque Dean's Cloister (1356) to the Deanery.

(10) To the N of the Deanery is the Winchester Tower.

(11) Between the Lower Ward and the Upper Ward is the Round Tower, built on an artificial mound in the time of Edward III. The uppermost section, 10 m (30 ft) high, was added in the reign of George IV. From the top (over 200 steps) there are extensive views.

(12) Immediately N of the Round Tower is the massive Norman Gateway.

(13) From the North Terrace there is a magnificent view of the Thames and of Eton (see entry) on the farther bank.

(14) The most northerly of the castle's towers is the Brunswick Tower.

(15) The State Apartments can be seen when the royal family is not in residence.

Near the entrance is a masterpiece of craftsmanship, the Queen's Dolls' House.

The main apartments are the following:

The Grand Staircase.

Charles II's Dining Room, with fine woodcarving by Grinling Gibbons, a splendid ceiling painting by Verrio (1678–80), a picture by van Dyck and period furniture.

The Rubens Room, with a series of works by Rubens.

The King's Closet, with a fine ceiling by Sir Jeffry Wyatville and pictures by Holbein, Rubens, Rembrandt, Dürer, Andrea del Sarto and Clouet.

The Queen's Closet, also with a ceiling by Wyatville and fine pictures.

The Picture Gallery, with a fine cornice by Grinling Gibbons and pictures by Holbein, van Dyck and William Dobson.

St George's Chapel

The Van Dyck Room (formerly the Queen's Ballroom), sumptuously appointed, with fine furniture and numerous paintings by van Dyck.

The Queen's Audience Chamber, with a notable ceiling painting by Verrio and Gobelins tapestries.

The Queen's Presence Chamber.

The Queen's Guard Chamber, with various historical relics.

St George's Hall, with the banners of the first 26 Knights of the Garter and thrones for the sovereign and his or her consort.

The Grand Reception Room.

The Grand Vestibule, with a valuable collection of arms and armour.

The Grand Entrance Hall, the oldest part of the State Apartments, with a fine vaulted roof (1363) and a valuable collection of drawings and cartoons by Leonardo da Vinci, Hans Holbein, Raphael and Michelangelo.

(16) In the Upper Ward is a fine statue of Charles II (1679).

(17) Along the E end of the Upper Ward are the Private Apartments.

The E end of the castle is defended by two towers:

(18) Prince of Wales Tower.

(19) Queen's Tower or Victoria Tower.

(20) Below the E end is the East Terrace.

(21, 22, 23) Along the S side of the Upper Ward are the Visitors' Apartments, with George IV's Gateway and Edward III's Tower.

(24) St George's Gateway leads into the Middle Ward.

(25, 26) Along the S side of the Lower Ward are Henry III's Tower and the Garter House and other premises belonging to the Military Knights of Windsor, an order of chivalry founded by Edward III.

To the S of the castle Windsor Great Park extends for a distance of some $5\frac{1}{2}$ miles.

Zoological Gardens   E1

The London Zoo, founded in 1826 by Sir Stamford Raffles and Sir Humphry Davy, has one of the finest collections of animals in the world, and is one of London's most popular attractions, attracting more than 2 million visitors a year. Run by the Zoological Society of London, it is also a research institution.

The Zoo is divided into three sections by the Regent's Canal (Grand Union Canal) and the Outer Circle, but the three parts are linked by three bridges over the canal and two pedestrian tunnels under the Outer Circle.

There are three entrances – the main entrance on the Outer Circle, the N entrance in Prince Albert Road, the S entrance in Broad Walk.

A particular attraction for children is the Children's Zoo with pony and donkey rides (in summer).

Address
Regent's Park, NW1

Underground stations
Baker Street, Regent's Park, Camden Town

Water-buses
Apr.–Oct.

Opening times
Beginning of Mar.–end of Oct., 9 a.m.–6 p.m., Sun. 9 a.m.–7 p.m.; Nov.–beginning of Mar. 10 a.m. to dusk.

Closed
25 Dec.

Admission charge

Practical Information A to Z

(Unless otherwise indicated, all telephone numbers given in this section are in the London telephone area: dialling code 01)

Air services

Airports	London's two principal airports are Heathrow, 22 km (14 miles) W of the city centre, and Gatwick, 48 km (30 miles) S. Two smaller airports, Luton in Bedfordshire and Stansted in Essex are largely used by charter flights.
	Heathrow and Gatwick provide connections with all parts of the world and with many towns in Britain.
Air terminals	British Caledonian Air Terminal, Victoria Station, London SW1. Underground station: Victoria. Reservations only; no check-in; open 24 hours a day.
Getting to and from Heathrow	There is a direct Underground link from central London (Piccadilly line) to Heathrow Central station, which is connected to the airport by a moving walkway. The journey between Piccadilly Circus and Heathrow takes about 45 minutes. Not suitable for passengers with heavy luggage.
	London Transport operates two express bus services linking Heathrow and central London. Route A1 (Heathrow–Cromwell Road–Hyde Park Corner–Victoria Station) operates at 20-minute intervals and takes about 60 minutes for the journey. Route A2 (Heathrow–Holland Park Avenue–Notting Hill Gate–Bayswater Road–Paddington Station) operates at half-hour intervals and takes about 50 minutes. Flat-rate fare £2.
	Green Line coaches 701, 704, 724, 726, 727, and 790 and London Transport buses 82, 105, 111, 140, 223, 285 and N97 (night) also serve Heathrow Central.
Getting to and from Gatwick	Gatwick is served by fast and frequent British Rail services between the airport and Victoria Station. Trains run at 15-minute intervals during the day (6 a.m.–midnight) and hourly during the night; the journey takes about 40 minutes. On certain trains special coaches are attached for airline passengers.
	Green Line coaches 727, 750, 755 and "Flightline" 777 (non-stop from Victoria) stop outside Gatwick terminal building.
Airline offices	British Airways 71 Regent Street, London W1. Victoria Terminal, Victoria, London SW1. West London Terminal, Cromwell Road, London SW7. Telephone enquiries: 370 5411 (West London Terminal).
	British Caledonian Airways, 193–194 Piccadilly, London W1. Tel. 668 4222.
	Pan Am, 193 Piccadilly, London W1. Tel. 409 0688.
	TWA, 200 Piccadilly, London W1. Tel. 636 4090.

Heathrow

Auction rooms

Two great London auction rooms in particular, Christie's and Sotheby's, occupy predominant positions in the world art market, making the headlines every now and then when some

A London auction

sensational new record price is achieved, such as the £2,300,000 paid for Rubens's "Samson and Delilah" at Christie's in July 1980. It is worth while attending one of their sales for the sake of the atmosphere alone. Potential purchasers can keep in touch with forthcoming sales by consulting the advertisements in "The Times" (on Tuesdays) or the "Telegraph" (Mondays) and applying for sale catalogues.

Banks

Banks are open Monday to Friday from 9.30 a.m. to 3.30 p.m. Money can also be changed at the airports and air terminals, in the larger hotels and in some of the big department stores – Harrods, Dickins and Jones, Selfridges, John Barker, Marks and Spencer (Marble Arch and Oxford Street).

Currency

The monetary unit of the United Kingdom is the pound sterling (£), which consists of 100 pence (p). There are Bank of England notes for £1, £5, £10, £20 and £50, and coins in denominations of ½p, 1p, 2p, 5p, 10p, 20p, 50p and £1. The ½p coin will shortly be withdrawn from circulation.

There are no restrictions on the import or export of either British or foreign currency, following the lifting of restrictions on the export of currency in October 1979.

Visitors from abroad are recommended to bring currency in the form of travellers' cheques or to use a Euro cheque card. The principal credit cards are widely accepted.

Changing foreign currency   See Banks

Customs regulations

Entering the country

Personal effects and holiday luggage, including sports gear, can be brought into the United Kingdom without payment of duty. In addition both visitors and British citizens can bring in, duty-free, specified quantities of alcohol (persons over 17 only), tobacco goods and perfume. Where these goods are obtained duty-free in the EEC or on a ship or aircraft, or outside the EEC, the allowances are 200 cigarettes or 100 cigarillos or 50 cigars or 250 grammes of tobacco (twice these amounts for persons who live outside Europe); 1 litre of alcoholic drinks over 22% vol. (38·8° proof) or 2 litres of alcoholic drinks not over 22% vol. (38·8° proof) or of fortified or sparkling wine, plus 2 litres of still table wine; 50 grammes (60 cc or 2 fluid ounces) or perfume and 250 cc (9 fluid ounces) of toilet water; together with other goods up to a value of £28. Where the goods are obtained duty and tax paid in the EEC the allowances are 300 cigarettes or 150 cigarillos or 75 cigars or 400 grammes of tobacco; 1½ litres of alcoholic drinks over 22% vol. (38·8° proof) or 3 litres of alcoholic drinks not over 22% vol. (38·8° proof), plus 4 litres of still table wine; 75 grammes (90 cc or 3 fluid ounces) of perfume and 375 cc (13 fluid ounces) of toilet water; and other goods up to a value of £120.

British banknote and coins

The import of certain goods is prohibited, including firearms and ammunition, flick knives, walkie-talkies, meat and poultry (unless fully cooked), certain plants and vegetables; live animals and birds are subject to restrictions (quarantine and rabies licence required for dogs, cats, etc.). Shotguns may be brought in without formalities for a period of up to 30 days (except in Northern Ireland).

There are restrictions on the export of antiques and paintings over 50 years old, firearms and ammunition, certain archaeological material, etc. Information from local offices of Customs and Excise (addresses in telephone directory).

Leaving the country

Emergencies

Fire, police, ambulance: dial 999. There is no charge for 999 calls.
If your car breaks down: see Motoring.

Events

For information about events in London consult the press (in particular the Friday supplement of "The Times" and the supplements of "The Sunday Times" and "The Observer") or periodicals like "What's On", "Time Out" (for younger people) or "Where to Go" (particularly for information on night life).

25 January: St Paul's Day; performance of Mendelssohn's oratorio "St Paul" in St Paul's Cathedral.

January

The Royal Tournament (July)

	30 January: Laying of wreaths on statue of Charles I in Trafalgar Square and service in Whitehall commemorating the "royal martyr".
February	**Ash Wednesday:** Stationers' Company service in crypt of St Paul's Cathedral, with members of the Company wearing traditional robes.
	Cruft's Dog Show, Olympia.
March	Chelsea Antiques Fair in Chelsea Town Hall (see entry). Boat Race (Oxford and Cambridge), on the Thames from Putney to Mortlake.
March/April	**Tuesday of Holy Week:** Performance of Bach's "St Matthew Passion" in St Paul's Cathedral.
	Maundy Thursday (Thursday of Holy Week): Royal Maundy ceremony, Westminster Abbey (in alternate years), at which the Queen, accompanied by the Royal Almoner and Yeoman of the Guard, distributes purses of specially minted Maundy money to a number of deserving men and women equal to the number of years in the Queen's age.
	Easter Day: Easter Parade in Battersea Park (a picturesque carnival parade, with horse-drawn carriages).
	Easter Monday: Procession and service in Westminster Abbey. Harness Horse Parade in Regent's Park.
May	**1 May:** Labour Day procession to Hyde Park (see entry).

Football Association Cup Final, Wembley Stadium.

(Late May/early June) Chelsea Flower Show, Royal Hospital, Chelsea.

24 June: Election of Sheriffs of City of London (an impressive ceremony in the Guildhall – see entry).

June

(Late June/early July) All England Lawn Tennis Championships, Wimbledon.

(2nd Saturday) Trooping the Colour on Horse Guards Parade on the Queen's official birthday.

Racing at Epsom.

Royal Ascot races.

Service of the Order of the Garter in St George's Chapel, Windsor, attended by the Queen, with a picturesque procession (first held in the 14th c.) of the Household Cavalry and Yeomen of the Guard.

Beginning of month: Procession of Vintners' Company, in traditional costumes, from Vintners' Hall to neighbouring churches.

July

Royal Tournament March Past on Horse Guards Parade: a colourful parade by all troops taking part in the Royal Tournament, held on the Saturday before the Tournament.

Royal Tournament, Earls Court (an impressive military display).

Opening of the Promenade Concerts (mid-July) for 8 weeks.

August

Promenade Concerts in Royal Albert Hall.

September

15 September (or near): Battle of Britain Day, with a fly-past over London (11 a.m.–noon).

Election of Lord Mayor.

Last night of Proms.

October

1st Sunday: Costermongers' Harvest Festival in St Martin-in-the-Fields at 3.30 p.m. An annual occasion, originating in the latter part of the 19th c., at which the London costermongers (the pearly kings and queens) are dressed in their traditional garb of jackets covered with pearly buttons.

21 October: Trafalgar Day, with a service and parade at Nelson's Column in Trafalgar Square (see entry).

Michaelmas (around 23 October): Payment of quit rents in the Royal Courts of Justice. An ancient traditional ceremony in which the City of London makes token payments to the Queen's Remembrancer by way of rent for two properties known as the Moors in Shropshire and the Forge in the parish of St Clement Danes (the situation of which is unknown). The rent for the Moors is an axe and a billhook, for the Forge six horseshoes and 61 nails.

November

State Opening of Parliament by the Queen (see Facts and Figures, Parliament).

1st Sunday: London to Brighton Veteran Car Run, starting from Hyde Park Corner.

5 November: Guy Fawkes Day, an occasion for firework displays commemorating Guy Fawkes's attempt to blow up Parliament on 5 November 1605 (the Gunpowder Plot).

2nd Friday: Admission of the Lord Mayor Elect. A colourful ceremony in which the outgoing Lord Mayor hands over the insignia of office to the new incumbent in the Guildhall.

2nd Saturday: Lord Mayor's Show. The new Lord Mayor drives in his state coach from the Guildhall to the Law Courts, where he is received by the Lord Chief Justice, representing the Crown.

December

Sunday before Christmas: Tower of London Church Parades. Parade and inspection of the Yeomen Warders in full-dress uniform before and after morning service.

26–28 December: Carol services in Westminster Abbey.

31 December: New Year's Eve celebrations, Trafalgar Square.

Galleries

In addition to the public and other art galleries open to the public there are numerous commercial galleries, most of them in Mayfair and St James's (e.g. in the side streets off New Bond Street) and in South Kensington. Even if you have no intention of buying anything you need not hesitate to go to one of their exhibitions: they are quite used to visitors who merely want to look at the pictures.

Information about such exhibitions can be obtained from advertisements in the press or from periodicals like "Time Out" and "What's On".

Hotels

Category	Tariff per night			
	1 person	2 persons	★★★★★	Luxury hotel
A	over £50	over £70	★★★★	Exceptionally well-appointed hotel
B	£30–50	£50–70	★★★	Well-appointed hotel
C	£20–30	£35–50	★★	High-standard hotel
D	£15–20	£22–35	★	Good hotel
E	£10–15	£15–22	☆	Specially built hotel
			★	Outstanding merit within normal star rating

Mayfair/Soho

★★★★★ Claridges, Brook Street, A, 205 r.
★★★★★ Connaught, Carlos Place, A, 90 r.
★★★★★ Dorchester, Park Lane, A, 280 r.
★★★★★ Grosvenor House, Park Lane, A, 478 r.
★★★★★ Hilton, Park Lane, A, 503 r.
★★★★★ Inn on the Park, Hamilton Place, Park Lane, A, 228 r.
★★★★★ Inter-Continental, 1 Hamilton Place, Hyde Park, A, 492 r.
★★★★★ May Fair, Stratton Street, B, 390 r.
★★★★★ Ritz, Piccadilly, A, 139 r.
★★★★ Athenaeum, Piccadilly, A, 112 r.
★★★★ Britannia, Grosvenor Square, A, 440 r.
★★★★ Brown's, Dover Street, A, 130 r.
★★★★ Cumberland, Marble Arch, A, 910 r.
★★★★ London Marriot, Grosvenor Square, B, 276 r.
★★★★ Park Lane, Piccadilly, A, 284 r.
★★★★ Piccadilly, Piccadilly, A, 290 r.
★★★★ St George's, Langham Place, A, 85 r.
★★★★ Selfridge Thistle, Orchard Street, A, 298 r.
★★★★ Westbury, New Bond Street, A, 256 r.
★★★ Chesterfield, 35 Charles Street, A, 85 r.
★★★ Mount Royal, Bryanston Street, B, 700 r.
★★★ Stratford Court, 350 Oxford Street, B, 139 r.
★★★ Washington, Curzon Street, B, 160 r.
★★ Green Park, Half Moon Street, B, 175 r.
★★ Regent Palace, Glasshouse Street, Piccadilly, C, 1068 r.
★★ Royal Augus, Coventry Street, C, 92 r.

Strand/Covent Garden/ Holborn

★★★★★ Savoy, Strand, A, 201 r.
★★★★ Russell, Russell Square, A, 318 r.
★★★★ Waldorf, Aldwych, A, 310 r.

Practical Information

☆☆☆	Bloomsbury Crest, Coram Street, Russell Square, B, 250 r.
★★★	Drury Lane Moat House, Drury Lane, A, 128 r.
★★★	Kingsley, Bloomsbury Way, C, 169 r.
★★★	Strand Palace, Strand, B, 761 r.
★★	Bedford Corner, Bayley Street, D, 85 r.
★★	Cora, Upper Woburn Place, C, 144 r.
★★	Grand, 126 Southampton Row, D, 92 r.

Victoria/Westminster/St James's

★★★★	Cavendish, Jermyn Street, A, 253 r.
★★★★	Duke's, St James's Place, A, 56 r.
★★★★	Goring, Beeston Place, Grosvenor Gardens, A, 100 r.
★★★★	Stafford, 16–18 St James's Place, A, 60 r.
☆☆☆	Royal Westminster Thistle, 49 Buckingham Palace Road, B, 135 r.
★★★	Royal Horseguards Thistle, Whitehall Court, B, 284 r.
★★★	Rubens, Buckingham Palace Road, C, 173 r.
★★★	Stakis St Ermin's, Caxton Street, B, 244 r.
★	Ebury Court, 26 Ebury Street, C, 39 r.

South Kensington/Earl's Court

☆☆☆☆	Forum Hotel London, Cromwell Road, B, 914 r.
★★★★	Gloucester, Harrington Gardens, A, 550 r.
☆☆☆☆	London International, 147 Cromwell Road, B, 413 r.
★★★	Barkston, 33–34 Barkston Gardens, B, 74 r.
★★★	Elizabetta, 162 Cromwell Road, C, 84 r.
★★★	Embassy House, 31–33 Queen's Gate, B, 70 r.
☆☆☆	Hogarth, Hogarth Road, D, 86 r.
★★★	Onslow Court, Queen's Gate, D, 146 r.
★★★	Rembrandt, Thurloe Place, D, 190 r.
★★	Leicester Court, 41 Queen's Gate Gardens, D, 67 r.

Kensington/ Knightsbridge

★★★★★	Berkeley, Wilton Place, A, 150 r.
★★★★★	Hyatt Carlton Tower, Cadogan Place, A, 228 r.
★★★★★	Hyde Park, Knightsbridge, A, 201 r.
★★★★★	Royal Garden, Kensington High Street, A, 427 r.
★★★★★	Sheraton Park Tower, 101 Knightsbridge, A, 293 r.
★★★★	Capital, Basil Street, A, 60 r.
★★★★	Kensington Close, Wright's Lane, B, 530 r.
★★★★	Kensington Palace Thistle, De Vere Gardens, B, 316 r.
☆☆☆☆	London Tara, Scarsdale Place (off Wright's Lane), C, 843 r.
☆☆☆	Holiday Inn Chelsea, 17–25 Sloane Street, A, 206 r.
★★★	Basil Street, Basil Street, B, 92 r.
★★★	Lowndes Thistle, Lowndes Street, A, 80 r.
☆☆☆	Royal Kensington, 380 Kensington High Street, B, 409 r.
★★	Hotel Lexham, 32–38 Lexham Gardens, D, 64 r.

Heathrow

☆☆☆☆	Ariel, Bath Road, Hayes, B, 178 r.
☆☆☆☆	Excelsior, Bath Road, West Drayton, A, 662 r.

☆☆☆☆	Heathrow Penta, Bath Road, Hounslow, A, 670 r.
☆☆☆☆	Holiday Inn, Stockley Road, West Drayton (no prices), 401 r.
☆☆☆☆	Sheraton-Heathrow, Colnbrook Bypass, West Drayton, B, 440 r.
☆☆☆	Berkeley Arms, Bath Road, Cranford, B, 42 r.
☆☆☆	Post House, Sipson Road, West Drayton, B, 594 r.
★★★	Skyway, Bath Road, Hayes, B, 445 r.

Markets

Chancery House, Chancery Lane, WC2.
Underground station: Chancery Lane.
Mon.–Fri. 9 a.m.–5.30 p.m., Sat. (except before public holidays) 9 a.m.–12.30 p.m.
40 shops selling period and modern silver, porcelain and ivories.

London Silver Vaults

King's Road, SW3.
Underground station: Sloane Square.
Mon. 10 a.m.–2 p.m., Tues.–Sat. 10 a.m.–6 p.m.
Large market with 110 stands; often overcrowded on Saturdays.

Chelsea Antiques Market

Islington, N1.
Underground station: Angel.
Mon.–Sat. 10.30 a.m.–5.30 p.m.
Antiques of the most varied kind and quality.

Camden Passage

High Road, SE10.
Underground station: New Cross or New Cross Gate, then 117 bus.
British Rail station: Greenwich.
Saturday.
Antiques of good quality.

Greenwich Antiques Market

Church Street.
Underground station: Edgware Road or Marylebone.
Tues.–Sat. 8 a.m.–6 p.m., Thurs. morning only.
An interesting junk market at which finds can be made. Best on Saturdays.

Church Street Market

Leather Lane, Holborn, EC1.
Underground station: Chancery Lane. Buses: 5, 8, 18, 22, 25, 45, 46, 55, 171, 243, 259, 501.
Mon.–Fri. 11 a.m.–3 p.m.
A large midday market near Hatton Garden.

Leather Lane Market

Middlesex Street, E1.
Underground stations: Liverpool Street, Aldgate, Aldgate East.
Sun. 9 a.m.–2 p.m.
London's most celebrated street market, noisy and swarming with humanity, including plenty of "characters". Here anything and everything can be bought, often at very reasonable prices. Best to get there before 11 to beat the crowds.

Petticoat Lane Market

Practical Information

Portobello Road Market

Portobello Road, W10.
Underground stations: Ladbroke Grove, Notting Hill Gate.
Mainly on Sat. 7 a.m.–6 p.m.
A combination of market and fair, with a continental touch; interesting clientele. Boutiques, antiques both genuine and fake, clothing. Daily market, but most interesting on Saturdays. The best bargains are to be had towards the end of the day, since many stallholders would rather reduce their prices to get rid of their goods than have to pack them up and take them home.

Motorail

There are some 30 Motorail services in Britain, conveying cars and passengers from London to western and northern England, Scotland and Wales and from Dover and Harwich and northern England and Scotland. Most services operate at night (car sleeper services). Information from travel agents, motoring organisations and British Rail offices.

Motoring

Driving in Britain

Most foreign visitors will require a little while to adjust themselves to driving on the left and overtaking on the right. Particular care should therefore be exercised in the early stages of a visit to Britain. Road signs and road markings are generally in line with international standards. Guidance on road traffic regulations and good driving practice is given in the "Highway Code", published by H.M. Stationery Office and available through the British Tourist Authority, motoring organisations and bookshops.

Speed limits

There is a speed limit of 112 km/h (70 m.p.h.) on motorways and roads with dual carriageway, 96 km/h (60 m.p.h.) on other roads and 48 km/h (30 m.p.h.) in built-up areas. Certain stretches of road may have other limits (often 64 or 80 km/h – 40 or 50 m.p.h.) indicated by signs.
Vehicles with trailers are subject to a speed limit of 80 km/h (50 m.p.h.), and are not allowed to use the third lane of a three-lane motorway.

Drink and driving

The maximum permitted blood alcohol level is 80 milligrammes of alcohol in 100 millilitres of blood.

Petrol

Petrol is normally sold by the gallon (4·546 litres), though most pumps are now calibrated to sell it by the litre; in such cases the petrol station is required to show both the gallon and the litre price. The quality (octane value) of the different grades is indicated by stars, from two to five in number.

The market, Portobello Road ▶

Practical Information

Tyre pressures

Tyre pressures are measured in pounds per sq. inch. Conversion to the continental system: see Weights and measures.

Motoring organisations

The two principal motoring organisations in Britain are the Automobile Association (AA) and the Royal Automobile Club (RAC):
Automobile Association,
Fanum House, Leicester Square, London WC2.
Information: tel. 954 7355.

Royal Automobile Club,
83–85 Pall Mall, London SW1.
Information: tel. 930 4343.

Breakdown assistance

Both the AA and the RAC run a breakdown service, available to their members and to members of affiliated foreign motoring organisations. In case of breakdown, repairs will either be carried out on the spot by the AA or RAC patrolman or the vehicle will be towed to the nearest garage.
To call for assistance in the London area:
AA: tel. 954 7373.
RAC: tel. (92) 33555 (N of Thames) or 681 3611 (S of Thames).

Emergency telephone

For police, fire or ambulance dial 999 anywhere in Britain.

Repair garages

The two motoring organisations maintain lists of garages handling all the well-known international makes of car.
Garages with a 24-hour service:
Belsize Garage,
27 Belsize Lane, London NW3.
Tel. 435 5472.
Cavendish Motors,
Cavendish Road, London NW6.
Tel. 459 0046.
Moon's Motors,
Kilburn High Road, London NW6.
Tel. 624 2323.

Music

Opera, concerts

London enjoys a high reputation for the quality of its musical life, with two opera-houses (the Royal Opera House and the English National Opera), six first-class symphony orchestras (Philharmonia Orchestra, London Symphony Orchestra, London Philharmonic Orchestra, Royal Philharmonic Orchestra, BBC Symphony Orchestra, Orchestra of the Royal Opera House) and a number of excellent chamber orchestras (Academy of St Martin-in-the-Fields, English Chamber Orchestra, London Bach Orchestra, etc.) and choirs (Philharmonia Chorus, Ambrosian Singers, Royal Choral Society, etc.).

St Martin's Lane, WC2, tel. 836 3161.
Underground station: Leicester Square.
This is the home of the English National Opera, with a first-class company and a repertoire which includes both classical and modern works.

Coliseum

Bow Street, WC2, tel. 240 1066.
Underground station: Covent Garden.
A world-famous opera-house with an equally famous ballet.
Information (24 hours a day): tel. 240 1911.

Royal Opera House, Covent Garden

An important element in London's musical life is the series of promenade concerts (the "Proms") held every year from July to September in the Albert Hall (see entry). The programmes range over the repertoire from the Baroque period to the present day. Tickets are reasonably priced, and the audiences are large and heterogeneous. Particularly popular is the "last night of the Proms", a traditional occasion on which the atmosphere is good-humoured and relaxed and the conductor becomes a kind of compère who has to maintain his hold over the audience as well as over the orchestra.

The Proms

London is the home of a number of world-famous ballets. The Royal Ballet and the London Festival Ballet specialise in the classical style, while the Ballet Rambert includes modern works in its repertoire and the London Contemporary Dance Theatre carries on the ideas of Martha Graham. There are also various experimental groups and workshops.

Dancing and ballet

Part of London's musical life and night life: jazz clubs

Practical Information

To find out what is on, read "Time Out" or "Melody Maker". Well known jazz clubs:

100 Club,
100 Oxford Street, W1.
Underground stations: Oxford Circus, Bond Street.
The best known basement club in London for traditional jazz. Admission charges vary according to the bands performing. Two bars and a small restaurant.

Half Moon,
93 Lower Richmond Road, SW15.
Underground station: Kew Gardens.
A pub with entertainments and jazz shows (mostly traditional). Entry charge.

Night life

The entertainment district best known to visitors is Soho; but its night spots and dives are hardly to be recommended to tourists (many clip-joints, much crude sex). The "in" districts and places vary from time to time: the once fashionable Carnaby Street has been overshadowed by Chelsea (particularly King's Road), while the district now gaining in popularity is Covent Garden (see entry).
For information about what is on consult the press or one of the periodicals like "Where to Go".

Opening hours

Banks

See Banks

Museums

Opening times vary widely, and no general rules can be laid down. See the entries for particular museums.
Most museums are closed on New Year's Day, Good Friday, the spring bank holiday (last Monday in May or first Monday in June), the summer bank holiday (last Monday in August or first Monday in September) and at Christmas. Before visiting a museum on one of these days, therefore, it is wise to ask the hotel porter or a tourist information office (see Tourist information).

Pubs

See Pubs

Shops

Most small shops are open from 9 a.m. to 5.30 p.m. Monday to Saturday. Some shops are closed on Saturday afternoon (e.g. Peter Jones in Sloane Square, Fortnum and Mason in Piccadilly and all Bond Street shops). Shops in the West End stay open until 7 p.m. on Thursdays; in the Knightsbridge, Sloane Square and King's Road areas they stay open until 7 p.m. on Wednesdays.

In the suburbs many shops have a weekly early closing day (usually Wednesday or Thursday) on which they close at 1 p.m.

Pets

For foreign visitors who think of bringing a dog or other pet to Britain for a short stay the advice must be "Don't!" Any animals brought into Britain are subject to a six months' quarantine period, and there are severe penalties (a prison sentence of up to a year and a fine of unlimited amount) for smuggling in animals illicitly. Rabies is unknown in Britain, and the object of these drastic measures is to keep it out.

Postal rates

Within the United Kingdom and to the Republic of Ireland: first class 16p, second class $12\frac{1}{2}$p (up to 60 g).
To Europe: $20\frac{1}{2}$p (up to 20 g). All letters to Europe go by air mail; air mail labels not necessary.
To the United States and Canada: air mail 28p (up to 10 g), surface mail $20\frac{1}{2}$p (up to 20 g).

Letters

Within the United Kingdom, the Republic of Ireland and Europe: as for letters.
To the United States and Canada: 26p.
Cards (including Christmas and birthday cards) addressed to countries outside the United Kingdom and the Republic of Ireland and containing no more than five words of conventional greeting can be sent as printed papers ($14\frac{1}{2}$p by surface mail to all countries, $20\frac{1}{2}$p by air mail to the United States and Canada).

Postcards

The post office in St Martin's Place, WC2 (Trafalgar Square, corner of William IV Street) is open 24 hours a day.

All-night post office

Pubs

The pub is a characteristic English institution where you can not only to get a glass of beer (or something stronger) but can also have a bite to eat. The standard of pub food has improved in recent years, and many pubs will often provide a better meal than a sandwich bar or many ordinary restaurants. In addition to sandwiches and sausages there may be such tasty dishes as cottage pie, steak and kidney pie or shepherd's pie. Some pubs even have table service.

Practical Information

Normally drinks are not served at the table. You go to the bar and ask for what you want, paying for it at once (no tip required).

Beer is ordered by the pint or half-pint (draught: i.e. from the cask or keg) or by the bottle. There are various kinds – bitter (the most popular), mild, mixed ("mild and bitter"), pale ale, brown ale (sweet and dark), stout (very dark, almost black) and lager (similar to the beer normally drunk in continental Europe). Most beer is served at room temperature; only lager is chilled.

Some pubs still have different rooms labelled "public bar", "saloon bar" and "private bar", dating from the time when workmen were segregated from the better class of customer and there was a special room for women. Nowadays these distinctions have lost their original significance.

NB: Children under 14 are not admitted to pubs.

Some of London's pubs are famous, others are known only to regular customers; some are of venerable antiquity, others are new and modern; some are elegant and fashionable establishments, others are modest and unpretentious places. A Londoner has his own favourite pub, where he feels at home and meets his friends: with some 16,000 pubs to choose from in London, visitors are presented with an embarrassingly wide range of choice.

Licensing hours

Public houses are usually open from 11 a.m.–3 p.m. and 5.30–11 p.m. on weekdays and from noon–2 p.m. and 7–10.30 p.m. on Sundays.

At the bar of a typical London pub

The Pub Information Centre,
93 Buckingham Palace Road, SW1.
Tel. 222 3232.
Open during office hours.

Information

Organised pub visits, starting from the Temple Underground
station, 7.30 p.m. on Fridays. Advance booking not necessary.
Information: Peter Westbrook, 3 Springfield Avenue, N10, tel.
883 2656.

Pub walks

Rail services

The Britrail Pass (obtainable only outside the United Kingdom)
gives visitors to Britain the freedom of the whole British railway
system at very reasonable cost. Available for a period of 8, 15 or
22 days or a month, it allows unlimited travel on all British Rail
services and on the Isle of Wight ferries. It can be supplemented
by the Britrail Sea Pass, which covers the crossing from and to
the Continent.

Britrail Pass

Rail Rover tickets, valid for either 7 or 14 days, cover travel over
the whole British Rail network or in a particular part of the
country.

Rail Rover tickets

Victoria Station

River launches

There are regular motor launch trips on the Thames from April to September – from Westminster Pier to Kew Gardens, Hampton Court and Richmond, from Charing Cross and Tower Pier to Greenwich. There are also combined rail and boat trips from Paddington and Waterloo stations to Windsor, Staines, Maidenhead, Marlow, Oxford, Henley and other places.

Information

London Tourist Board, River Boat Information Service, tel. 730 4812.
British Tourist Authority (see Tourist information).
Thames Launches Ltd, Charing Cross Pier, Victoria Embankment, WC2, tel. 930 0921 (Tower/Greenwich only).

Shopping

London is famous for its departmental stores and specialist shops; for visitors from abroad it has always been a shopping Mecca with a great number of shopping districts.
There are three main shopping areas of interest to visitors. The first extends W from Tottenham Court Road and Charing Cross Road, taking in Oxford Street, Regent Street and Bond Street and extending S to Piccadilly and Jermyn Street. The second

Sightseeing launches on the Thames ▶

Oxford Street, one of London's great shopping streets

includes Knightsbridge, Brompton Road and Fulham Road, Sloane Street and King's Road. The third is centred on Kensington High Street and Kensington Church Street.

For fuller information about shops and shopping in London, consult the British Tourist Authority's pocket guide, "Shopping in London", or the "London Shopping Guide" published by Penguin Books.

Shop hours

See Opening hours

Department stores

Among the most famous of London's many fine department stores are Harrods, Liberty's and Fortnum and Mason.

Harrods,
Brompton Road, SW1.
Underground station: Knightsbridge.
Harrods, the largest store in London and perhaps in Europe, has the appropriate motto "Everything for everybody everywhere" ("Omnia omnibus ubique") and telegraphic address "Everything London". This is scarcely an overstatement, for Harrods does indeed seem to have everything, including a bank, a funeral parlour, a zoo and the largest piano department in the world. You can insure yourself in Harrods, hire a Rolls Royce or have suitcases tailored to fit into the boot of your car; you can buy theatre tickets in Harrods, book a holiday, arrange a party or a wedding or hire a butler.

Liberty and Co.,
Regent Street, W1.
Underground station: Oxford Circus.

Harrods ("Everything London")

Liberty's

Fortnum and Mason

Liberty's, like Harrods, is one of the sights of London, with its exuberant half-timbered exterior. The main building is in Great Marlborough Street. The interior is in the style of a vast Tudor palace.

Fortnum and Mason,
Piccadilly, W1.
Underground stations: Piccadilly Circus, Green Park.
Fortnum and Mason, the most exclusive of London's department stores – the male staff wear formal dark suits with striped trousers – is notable mainly for its food department. The officers of Wellington's army were supplied by Fortnum and Mason, and the shop still has the Royal Warrant as a supplier to the Queen.

Sightseeing tours

By bus

The easiest way of seeing London is by bus – either on your own, using the ordinary service buses (with an excellent view from the top deck), or on an organised sightseeing tour.

Red Bus Rover ticket

A Red Bus Rover ticket allows you to use any of the red London Transport buses for one whole day. You can buy your ticket at any London Transport travel information centre (see Tourist information), at most Underground stations and at bus garages (9 a.m.–7 p.m. only), at London Tourist Board information centres or from agents of National Travel.

London Explorer ticket

A London Explorer ticket gives you the same freedom to use any London bus (and most of the Underground) for a period of 1, 3, 4 or 7 days.

Round London Sightseeing Tour

This tour, run by London Transport, is an excellent and inexpensive way of getting a first general impression of London. There is no guide, but passengers are given a free souvenir map which shows what to look for on the way. The tours start from Piccadilly Circus, Marble Arch (near Speakers' Corner) and Victoria (Grosvenor Gardens), leaving at least once hourly from 9 a.m.–8 p.m. in summer (March–October) and from 9 a.m.–4 p.m. in winter (October–March, except on 25 December). Seats are not bookable.

London Transport Guided Tours

London Transport also runs coach tours (with a guide) in London and to places of interest around London. All prices include admission charges, and on most tours lunch or tea as well. It is best to book in advance – at any London Transport travel information centre (see Tourist information) or at Victoria Coach Station.

Evan Evans Tours

This firm runs tours of London in the mornings and of the surrounding area in the afternoons. If you join the tour at Tottenham Court Road or Russell Square advance booking is not necessary; if you are joining at any other point on the route a ticket must be obtained in advance from one of the booking offices mentioned below or from the London Tourist Board information centre at Victoria Station (near platform 15).

Booking offices and departure points:
Evan Evans (with waiting room and toilets),
Metropolis House, 41 Tottenham Court Road, W1, tel. 637
4171.
Underground stations: Tottenham Court Road, Goodge Street.
Passenger Reception Centre,
72–74 Russell Square, WC1.
Underground station: Russell Square.

Passengers are picked up at the following hotels: London
Hilton, Penta House, Kensington Hilton, Royal Kensington,
Cumberland, West Centre, Cunard International.

Tours of London in the morning, of the surrounding area in the
afternoon. Advance booking advisable.
Leaflets describing the tours are available. Tel. 837 3111 (day
and night).

Frames Tours

Booking:
Frames House, 46 Albemarle Street, W1, tel. 493 3181.
Whiteley's, Queensway, W2, tel. 229 1234.
17 Woburn Place, WC1, tel. 837 2254–5.
Sightseeing and Coach Hire Department, 11 Herbrand Street,
WC1, tel. 837 6311.
London Tourist Board, Victoria Station (platform 15).

Principal departure points:
Frames, 11 Herbrand Street, WC1 (Underground: Russell
Square).
17 Woburn Place, Russell Square, WC1 (Underground:
Russell Square).
Seymour Street, W1 (corner of Edgware Road, near Marble
Arch; Underground: Marble Arch).

Half-day and whole-day tours are run by:
American Express, 6 Haymarket, SW1, tel. 930 4411.
Thomas Cook, 45 Berkeley Street, W1, tel. 491 7434 and 499
4000.
Seats can also be booked through the London Tourist Board,
Victoria Station (platform 15).

Other coach tours

A number of organisations operate guided walks, lasting
perhaps 1½ hours, which are an excellent way of getting to
know London intimately and which take visitors into parts of
the city with which even Londoners are not familiar.

Sightseeing on foot

London Walks,
139 Conway Road, Southgate, N14, tel. 882 2763.
Walks around places of historical interest, at weekends
throughout the year and also during the week in summer
(May–October). Also pub walks throughout the year.

This sightseeing trail was laid out on the occasion of the
Queen's Silver Jubilee in 1977, and takes in all the main sights
of London. The route is marked by metal discs on the

Silver Jubilee Walkway

pavement, but to avoid any danger of losing your way it is as well to obtain the route map published by the London Tourist Board.

Canalside walks

These towpath walks along the Regent's Canal and Grand Union Canal provide some unusual viewpoints on London. Opening times vary according to the time of year, but the walks are always closed at dusk. (Information on opening times from the London Tourist Board, see Tourist information.) Children under 10 are not admitted unless accompanied by an adult. Bicycles are not permitted.

Lisson Grove, NW1, to Muriel Street, N1, passing London Zoo and Camden Lock.
Underground stations: Marylebone, King's Cross.

Vincent Terrace, N1, to Wharf Road, N1, passing the City Basin.
Underground station: Angel.

Harrow Road, W9, to Kensal Rise, W10.
Underground stations: Warwick Avenue, Kensal Green.

Taxis

Taxis can be hailed in the street (if the "Taxi" or "For hire" sign on the roof is illuminated, indicating that it is free), hired at a taxi-rank or called by telephone.
The telephone numbers of taxi-ranks are listed under "Taxicab" in the London telephone directory.
Radio taxis can be called by ringing 286 6010, 286 4848.

Fares

The current tariff is displayed in the taxi. The fare payable is shown on the meter, which the driver must bring into operation at the beginning of the journey. The meter also shows extra charges for additional passengers and luggage carried outside, as listed in the tariff.

Taxi-drivers are not obliged to accept fares (passengers) for journeys of over 6 miles, or over 20 miles from Heathrow Airport. If they do the fare is as shown on the meter, except when the destination is outside Greater London, when the fare must be agreed in advance.

Complaints

Complaints should be addressed to the Public Carriage Office, 15 Penton Street, London N1, tel. 278 1744.

Minicabs

Minicabs are ordinary cars operating a form of taxi service and can be hired only by telephone. There is no advantage in hiring them for short journeys, since they are cheaper than taxis of the traditional type only where the distance to be travelled is over two miles.
In general the police warn passengers against using minicabs; but most hotels and pubs have the telephone number of a

minicab firm with which they have regular dealings and which has normally proved reliable.

At least 20p for a short journey, otherwise 15–20%.

Tipping

Telephoning

The dialling code for London is 01. It should be dialled only when calling from outside London.

London dialling code

In case of difficulty in making a call the operator can be called by dialling 100.

Calling the operator

There are two types of public telephone (pay-phone), the older type with a dial and the new type with press-buttons (blue pay-phones). Both types are coin-operated, the coins accepted by the coin-box being indicated in a notice above the telephone. Before making a call be sure that you have enough coins of the right denominations.

Using public telephones

In this type the coins are inserted after the number you are calling is answered.
To make a call, lift the handset and listen for the dialling tone (a continuous purring or high-pitched hum). When you hear it, dial the number (or code and number) you want to call, and listen for the ringing tone (a repeated burr-burr sound). When the call is answered the ringing tone will change to the pay-tone (a series of rapid pips), and you must then insert a coin or coins. To continue a call, insert more money either during the conversation or immediately you hear the pay-tone again.

Dial pay-phones

In the blue pay-phone the money must be inserted before the call is made. These pay-phones have a minimum call charge higher than the value of the smallest coin accepted.
To make a call, lift the handset and listen for the dialling tone; when it comes on the credit display will flash. Insert money (at least the minimum call charge) until the flashing stops; the value of the money inserted will then appear on the credit display. Then dial the number you want; if the dialling tone stops before you start to dial, press the blue follow-on call button, listen for the dialling tone and then dial the number again. Listen for the ringing tone and speak when you are connected. To continue a call, insert more money either during the conversation or when you hear the pay-tone.
If your call fails, or you want to make another call with your remaining credit, do not replace the handset but press the blue follow-on button and dial again.
At the end of your call any unused coins will be returned. (No change is given for coins partly used.)

Press-button pay-phones

Underground station: St James's Park. Buses: 10, 11, 24, 29, 70, 76, 149, 503, 507.
This bureau is specially equipped to handle long-distance calls (direct connections with 85 countries). It does not accept collect (reversed charge) calls. It is a convenient place from which to make calls of some length if you have no access to a private telephone.

Westminster International Telephone Bureau

Practical Information

Telephoning telemessages — Dial 100.

Special services — Speaking clock: 123.
Directory enquiries, London: 142.
Directory enquiries, outside London: 192.
Weather, London: 246 8091.
Road conditions within 50 miles of London: 246 8021.
Teletourist (events of the day): 246 8041.
Children's London (events for children): 246 8007.

Theatres

With more than 60 theatres, London offers a varied dramatic spectrum, ranging from performances of the great theatrical classics to avant-garde and experimental productions and theatre workshops. In addition to world-famous establishments such as the National Theatre and the Royal Shakespeare Company (housed in the new Barbican Arts Centre) there are many smaller houses offering experimental plays, amateur performances, workshops and political theatre. Some theatres, such as the Royal Court, specialise in plays by contemporary authors, while others stick to a well-tried formula, including Agatha Christie's "Mousetrap", which has beaten all box office records with a run approaching its thirtieth year.

To find out what is on, consult the press or one of the periodicals like "What's On", "Time Out" or "Where to Go". There are no performances on Sundays.

A performance by the Royal Shakespeare Company

It is advisable to book seats in advance, since there is usually a great demand for tickets. This can be done either at the theatre box office or through a ticket agency (which will usually charge a commission of perhaps 25%). The following is a selection of agencies:

Keith Prowse, 24 Store Street, WC1, tel. 836 2184.

Abbey Box Office, 27 Victoria Street, SW1, tel. 222 2992.

H. J. Adams, 5 Grosvenor Street, W1, tel. 493 8311; 211 Baker Street, NW1, tel. 486 2996.

Albermarle Booking Agency, 13 Liverpool Street, EC2, tel. 283 5314.

Army and Navy Stores, 105 Victoria Street, SW1, tel. 834 1234.

Cecil Roy, 74 Old Brompton Road, SW7, tel. 589 0211.

Edwards and Edwards, Palace Theatre, Shaftesbury Avenue, W1, tel. 734 9761.

Fenchurch Booking Agency, 94 Southwark Street, SE1, tel. 928 8585.

Lacon and Ollier, 60 South Audley Street, W1, tel. 499 3631.

G. S. Lashmar, 18 South Molton Street, W1, tel. 493 4731.

Leader and Co., 13–14 Royal Arcade, Old Bond Street, W1, tel. 629 7097.

Premier Box Office, 188 Shaftesbury Avenue, WC2, tel. 240 2245.

Rakes Ticket Agency, 31 Coventry Street, W1, tel. 240 0681.

Webster and Waddington, 74 Mortimer Street, W1, tel. 580 3030.

Time

Britain observes Greenwich Mean Time (GMT) or Western European Time, which is 1 hour behind Central European Time and 5 hours ahead of New York time.

British Summer Time (BST), 1 hour in advance of GMT, is in force from the latter part of March to the latter part of October. Although the 24-hour clock is used in railway timetables, etc., the 12-hour reckoning of time (1 a.m. to 12 noon, 1 p.m. to 12 midnight) is the one generally used,

Tipping

Cloakroom: 20p.

Hairdresser: 10–15%.

Hotels: included in bill.

Pubs: 10–15% for table service; no tip for service at bar.

Restaurants: 10–15%.

Taxis: at least 20p for a short journey, otherwise 15–20%.

Toilets: 10p for a clean towel and service.

Tourist information

Information can be obtained from offices of the British Tourist Authority and British Rail.

Outside Britain

The visitor to London is well served by tourist information offices with knowledgeable and helpful staff. They stock a

In London

wide range of useful leaflets, maps and plans, brochures and guides of all kinds. One of the most attractive and useful books on London is "The Book of London", published by the Automobile Association.

British Tourist Authority (BTA)

64 St James's Street, SW1A 1NF, tel. 499 9325.
Underground station: Green Park
Open Mon.–Fri. 9 a.m.–6 p.m., Sat. 9 a.m.–12.30 p.m. (until 4.30 p.m. in summer).
Information on the whole of Britain. Free brochures; other material on sale.
A particularly useful BTA publication is "London: Your Sightseeing Guide" (£1.20).

London Tourist Board

Head office, 26 Grosvenor Gardens, SW1, tel. 730 0791.

Tourist Information Centres

Victoria Station (near platform 15).
Underground station: Victoria.
Open daily May–Sept., 7.45 a.m.–10.15 p.m., Oct.–April, 9 a.m.–8.30 p.m.
Tourist information, leaflets, accommodation booking service; wide range of guide books, touring maps, posters and slides; tourist tickets for bus and Underground, sightseeing tour tickets.

Heathrow Central Station, Heathrow Airport.
Open daily 8 a.m.–7.30 p.m.; extended hours July–August.
Tourist information, leaflets, accommodation booking service.

Selfridges, Oxford Street, W1.
Underground station: Bond Street.
Ground floor. Open during shop hours.

Harrods, Knightsbridge, SW1.
Underground station: Knightsbridge.
Fourth floor. Open during shop hours.

Telephone information service: 730 0791 (Mon.–Fri. 9 a.m.–5.30 p.m.).
Teletourist (recorded, 24 hours a day: events of the day): 246 8041.
Children's London (events for children): 246 8007.
Dial an Exhibition (details of museums and art galleries): 730 0977.

Useful booklets published by the London Tourist Board:
"London is . . . for Children" (47p).
"London is . . . Weekends" (47p).
"London – a Guide for Disabled Visitors" (£1.20).

City of London Information Centre

St Paul's Churchyard, EC4, tel. 606 3030.
Underground station: St Paul's.
Open April–September, Mon.–Fri. 9.30 a.m.–5 p.m., Sat. 10 a.m.–4 p.m.; October–March, Mon.–Sat. 10 a.m.–12.30 p.m., closed Sun. and public holidays.
Leaflets, maps, books, information.

Head office, 55 Broadway, SW1H 0BD, tel. 222 1234.
Underground station: St James's Park.
Open Mon.–Fri. 10.15 a.m.–5 p.m.

London Transport

Griffith House, 280 Old Marylebone Road, NW1.
Underground: Edgware Road.
Open Mon.–Fri. 9 a.m.–4 p.m.

Travel Information Centres
(in Underground stations):
Piccadilly Circus: open daily 8.30 a.m.–9.30 p.m.
Euston: open daily 8.30 a.m.–9.30 p.m.
King's Cross: open daily 8.30 a.m.–9.30 p.m.
Victoria: open daily 8.30 a.m.–9.30 p.m.
St James's Park: open Mon.–Fri. 8.30 a.m.–6.30 p.m.
Oxford Circus: open Mon.–Sat. 8.30 a.m.–9.30 p.m., Sun. 8.30
a.m.–6 p.m.
Heathrow Central: open daily 7.30 a.m.–9.30 p.m.

Telephone enquiries: 222 1234 (24-hour service).

Useful London Transport publications:
"Visitor's London" (£1.75).
"Getting There" (95p).
"London's Museums and Art Galleries" (45p).
"Theatre London" (£3.25).

British Rail Travel Centre,
12 Regent Street, SW1.
Underground station: Piccadilly Circus.
Open Mon.–Fri. 9 a.m.–5 p.m.
Information, tickets and reservations for all rail journeys in the
United Kingdom and to Ireland and the Continent. Personal
callers only.

British Rail

National Express,
Victoria Coach Station, Buckingham Palace Road, SW1, tel.
730 0202.
Underground station: Victoria.
Open daily 8 a.m.–10 p.m.
Information on coach services throughout the country.

National Travel (NBC) Ltd

Eccleston Bridge, Victoria, SW1, tel. 834 6563.
Underground station: Victoria.
Open daily 8.30 a.m.–5.30 p.m.
Information on Green Line and London Country Bus services.

Victoria Station (kiosk at platform 8), tel. 834 3925.
Underground station: Victoria.
A service, manned by volunteers, which helps foreign visitors
who have lost their passport, their money or their luggage. It
will also help in other emergencies. Mainly intended for young
people (au pairs, schoolchildren, students) and mothers with
young children.

International Travellers' Aid

146 Great Western Road, W11, tel. 229 8219.
Underground station: Westbourne Park.
A friendly information service on all aspects of the "alternative
society". Particularly helpful in finding cheap accommodation
in an emergency.

B.I.T.

A pedestrian tunnel in the Underground

Underground

The Underground ("Tube") is the quickest way of getting about in central London. The trains travel fast and run at frequent intervals from 5.30 a.m. to midnight (on Sundays to shortly before midnight). The time between stations averages about 2 minutes; changing trains at a junction station takes about 5 minutes. Some stations are closed on Sundays and a few also on Saturdays.

The rush hours (between 8 and 10 in the morning, between 4.30 and 6.30 in the evening) should be avoided if possible.

Fares

Fares vary with the distance travelled. A list of fares is displayed in the ticket hall of every Underground station. Return tickets are worth while only for journeys of some length. After 10 a.m. cheap day returns are available.

Tickets can be bought either from a ticket machine or at the ticket office. They must be shown to the collector at the gate or, in the case of yellow tickets issued at stations with automatic gates, inserted in the slot at the entrance. As you pass through the automatic gate remember to take your ticket from the slit on top of the gate. Tickets must be retained throughout the journey and given up to the collector at the exit gate.

Before travelling, work out your route on the Underground plan at the end of this Guide. A large-scale plan is displayed in the ticket hall of every Underground station. Once past the gate, follow the signs for the line you want: the best plan is to note the station at the end of the line as well as the name (and the distinctive colour) of the line. From some platforms trains leave for a number of different stations; in such cases make sure that you get the right one by watching the illuminated indicator above the platform or on the front of the train.

On most Underground trains the doors are opened by the guard. Some new trains on the District line have doors which the passenger must open by pressing a button.

London Explorer tickets, which can be bought at any Underground station and at London Transport travel information centres (see Tourist information), are issued for periods of 1, 3, 4 or 7 days and allow unlimited travel on most of the Underground system (excluding only stations beyond Northwood, Harrow and Wealdstone and Woodford on the Epping line) and on all London buses.

London Explorer tickets

A central Tube Rover ticket allows unlimited travel for one day between more than 50 stations in central London. They can be bought at any Underground station or London Transport travel information centre in the Central Tube Rover area and at London Tourist Board information centres.

Central Tube Rover tickets

Holders of London Explorer and Central Tube Rover tickets enjoy reductions on London Transport's sightseeing tours.

Weights and measures

Visitors from countries using the metric system will need to get used to the British (Imperial) weights and measures.

1 inch = 2·54 cm	1 cm = 0·39 in.	Length
1 foot = 30·48 cm	10 cm = 0·33 ft	
1 yard = 91·44 cm	1 m = 1·09 yd	
1 mile = 1·61 km	1 km = 0·62 mile	

1 square inch (in²) = 6·45 cm²	1 cm² = 0·155 in²	Area
1 square foot (ft²) = 9·288 dm²	1 dm² = 0·108 ft²	
1 square yard (yd²) = 0·836 m²	1 m² = 1·196 yd²	
1 square mile (mi²) = 2·589 km²	1 km² = 0·386 mi²	
1 acre = 0·405 ha	1 ha = 2·471 acres	

1 pint = 0·568 litre	1 litre = 1·76 pints	Volume (liquids)
1 gallon = 4·546 litres	10 litres = 2·20 gallons	
(Note that the US pint and gallon are equivalent to 0·83 Imperial pint or gallon.)		

1 ounce (oz) = 28·35 g	100 g = 3·527 oz	Weight
1 pound (lb) = 453·59 g	1 kg = 2·205 lb	
1 stone (14 lb) = 6·35 kg	10 kg = 1·57 stones	

1 lb/in² = 0·07 kg/cm²	1 kg/cm² = 14·2 lb/in²	Pressure
20 lb/in² = 1·41 kg/cm²	1·5 kg/cm² = 21·3 lb/in²	
30 lb/in² = 2·1 kg/cm²	2 kg/cm² = 28·4 lb/in²	

	Ladies					Men						Clothing sizes
Continental	36	38	40	42	44	46	48	50	52	54	56	
British	32	34	36	38	40	36	38	40	42	44	46	

Useful Telephone Numbers at a Glance

Fire, police, ambulance		999
Airlines		
British Airways		370 5411
British Caledonian		668 4222
Pan Am		409 0688
TWA		636 4090
Airports (flight information)		
Heathrow		759 7702–4
		759 7115–7
	after 10 p.m.	759 7432
Gatwick		(0293) 31299
Breakdown assistance		
Automobile Association		954 7373
Royal Automobile Club (N of Thames)		(92) 33555
(S of Thames)		681 3611
Car ferries		
Sealink		834 2345
Seaspeed		606 3681
Townsend Thoresen		437 7800
Prins Ferries		734 4431
Events (Teletourist)		246 8041
Events for children (Children's London)		246 8007
Lost property		
Britisth Rail, Eastern region		837 4200
Western region		723 7040
Southern region		928 5151
Green Line and London Country Bus services		(74) 42411
Radio taxis		286 6010
		286 4848
		272 3030
Telegrams, inland		190
Telegrams, foreign		193
Telephones		
Directory enquiries, London		142
outside London		192
Tourist information		
London Tourist Board (Mon.–Fri. 9 a.m.–5.30 p.m.)		730 0791
London Transport (24-hour service)		222 1234
City of London		606 3030

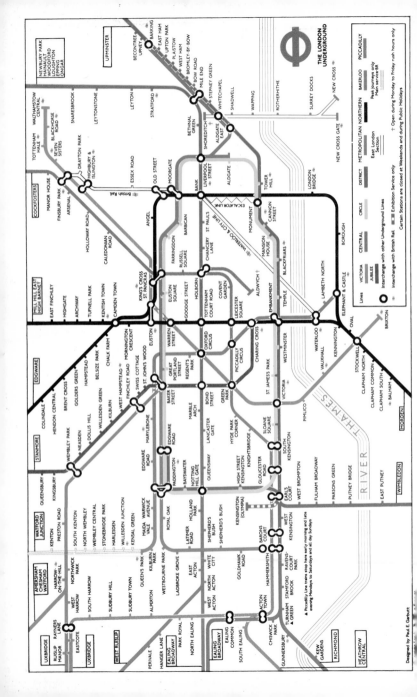